POWER PROMOTING

POWER PROMOTING

How to Market Your Business to the Top!

Jeffrey Sussman

John Wiley & Sons, Inc.

New York • Chichester • Weinheim • Brisbane • Singapore • Toronto

Library of Congress Cataloging in Publication Data:
Sussman, Jeffrey.
    Power promoting : how to market your business to the top! /
Jeffrey Sussman.
      p. cm.
    Includes bibliographical references.
    ISBN 0-471-14254-9 (pbk. : alk. paper)

    1. Marketing.   2. Sales promotion. I. Title.
    HF5415.S9168 1997
    658.8–dc20   96-13043

Printed in the United States of America

10 9 8 7 6 5 4 3 2 1

To my wife and best friend, Barbara

To my mother and stepfather, Flora and Donald

To Eileen and Tom

For my niece, Katie:
a future filled with success, fulfillment, and happiness

In memory of Peter Ramsay

Acknowledgments

There are few editors as charming, humorous, insightful, and helpful as Ruth Mills. She is not only a fine editor, but a woman whose friendship I value.

I owe a debt of gratitude to Michael Cohn, who suggested that I contact Ruth Mills. He is an agent by profession, but a thoughtful friend by inclination.

Numerous clients have given me the experiences I needed to write this book. I cannot thank them all, but I would be remiss not to express my appreciation to Stephen J. Cabot, Len Feldman, and Jerry Palace.

And finally, my thanks to Tom D'Amico, mapmaker and navigator.

Contents

INTRODUCTION

Your Business and This Book

Are you about to start a business? Have you recently started a business that isn't doing as well as it should? Do you have a business that was once successful but is now suffering from diminishing sales and profits?

If you answered "yes" to any of these questions, this book can help you achieve success and turn around a business that is failing. It will show you how to think creatively about promoting your business, and how to turn promotions into increased sales and profits. In addition, it offers lessons on becoming your own publicist: you will learn how to use publicity as a valuable marketing tool. By example and prescription, this book will help you to promote your business.

In fact, this book will show you how you can use the kinds of methods that large companies use to promote their products and/or services. While large companies spend millions of dollars on such promotions, the promotions in this book will cost you comparatively little. For years, my clients have been spending anywhere from a hundred dollars to several thousand dollars on individual promotions to market their successful businesses!

When you have finished reading this book and mastered its lessons, you will be well on your way to achieving new levels of success. Even if you have little or no training in marketing and public relations, you can learn to be an effective promoter of your business.

In fact, if you have an entrepreneurial spirit and great business ideas, but little expertise in turning your ideas into marketing promotional successes, this book will help you to execute promotions that get profitable results.

WHAT'S INSIDE

This book will help you reach your goals by explaining how to identify your markets. Both conventional and unconventional markets are targeted. Next, it teaches how to compete with others who are selling the same products/services.

Following chapters give examples and prescriptions for promoting your business. You will learn how to create provocative press releases that get results; which media to target, including both trade and consumer; and how to set up media interviews and how to conduct yourself during such interviews.

Once news and/or feature stories appear, you will learn how to market that publicity through direct mail campaigns that include reprints, solicitation letters, Rolodex cards, and brochures. I will explain how to buy a targeted mailing list. In addition, you will learn how to write, publish, and distribute marketing-oriented newsletters, and how to create brochures and solicitation letters that get results. Once the direct mail process has been completed, you will learn how to write telephone marketing scripts and make follow-up phone calls, or hire college students to make scripted phone calls.

Once new business has been acquired, you will learn how to promote that new business to get even more business. In fact, you will learn how to maintain this process for as long as you are in business.

You will also learn how to use coupons, how to cross-promote your products/services, how to participate with other businesses in joint promotions, how to create tie-ins with related products/services, how to barter for free advertising, how to create media events, how to work with well-known charities to promote your business by generating charitable income, and how to put together contests that get media attention and promote sales. For example, I organized an unusual contest for my foot-care client. It was called The Most Beautiful Feet in America Contest. More than 400 women showed up at a hotel ballroom to show off their tootsies, each hoping to win a one-year foot modeling contract. The winner's feet appeared on product packages and in-store posters. Since feet had never been the subject of a beauty contest, we got a foot up in a new area. The result was an extraordinary amount of publicity that included international coverage by *CNN*, local and regional television news coverage, syndicated newspaper columns, national magazines, trade magazines, and dozens of daily newspapers. People were invited to send a self-addressed, stamped, #10 envelope to us, and we mailed each of them a brochure of tips for fit feet and a $3-off discount coupon for the purchase of any two foot-care products! Not only was the media coverage dramatic, but sales jumped just as dramatically too.

No matter what you are trying to sell, there are always new and unusual ways to market and promote it!

In addition, I will explain how to put on seminars at no cost to yourself, and what kinds of trade shows, exhibits, and fairs to participate in; how to create grand openings that resemble Hollywood premieres; and how to sell items that will further market your products/services such as t-shirts, toys, and other premium incentives. I will even explain how to host a media contest for celebrity look-alikes, and how to raise money for local charities so that you will benefit from "doing good." Altogether, this book will provide you with a complete and, in some instances, adventurous blueprint for reaching the largest possible customer base.

WHY I CAN HELP YOU PROMOTE YOUR BUSINESS

In a career that has spanned more than twenty-five years, I have helped virtually every kind of business—from manufacturers to service businesses—reach new levels of success. In addition, I have owned and operated a wide assortment of businesses, including an art gallery, a day camp, a publishing company, a book store, a health club, a gymnastics school, and—of course—a marketing and public relations firm. For several years, I have also been teaching two marketing and promotion courses at The New School for Social Research in New York City.

I feel especially qualified to help you not only because I have operated my own businesses, but because I have also succeeded in promoting the businesses of others. Indeed, my combined experiences have given me the requisite skills and perspective for helping others.

In addition, I had worked for several marketing and public relations agencies for many years before I decided to open my own agency. I decided, perhaps as you have, that I no longer wanted to work for others and no longer wanted to waste my time in office politics. Like you, I decided to chart my own course.

While working for other marketing and public relations agencies, I acquired the necessary skills to promote both large and small companies. I learned valuable lessons while working on behalf of some very large companies and trade associations: Kentucky Fried Chicken, Direct Mail Marketing Association, Hueblein, Nissan, Mattel Electronics, several movie studios, The Sole Leather Council, The Mexican Tourist Bureau, The Concorde airplane, The City of New York, various politicians (Bella Abzug and Ed Koch, among others), Bertolli Olive Oil, Ronzoni Spaghetti, Perugina Chocolates, The World Almanac & Book of Facts, Dino DeLaurentis Foods, The Neighborhood Cleaners' Association, and various others.

By the time I opened my own company, I had discovered that no other marketing and public relations agencies were specializing in small to mid-size companies. Such companies, with their limited funds, cannot afford the hefty retainers of $3,000 to $10,000 a month that large agencies routinely charge. I decided to keep my overhead low, and charge retainers that small to mid-size businesses could afford.

Thus far, I have helped numerous clients attain new levels of success, and I have helped others as a teacher. Now I want to help thousands more through this book. More than half of all businesses fail within their first five years. If I can help reduce that mortality rate, I will have performed a useful service, and achieved my own kind of success.

LEARN FROM MY CLIENTS' SUCCESSES

Here are some examples of the kinds of clients that I have helped. They represent a wide range of professional services, manufacturing, wholesale distribution, and retail businesses.

Mr. Foot Care: I helped a foot-care products company go from being a successful mail-order company to being one of the leading distributors of foot-care products sold in major retail outlets! In fact, after three years, my client's products were in every drugstore chain, every mass-market retailer, and every superstore—not just in the United States, but in countries all over the globe! As if that were not enough, my client was also able to capture 15% of the Japanese foot-care market! Not bad for a mid-size American company.

The president of the company contacted me in 1990, and I put together a marketing and public relations program for him. The bare-bones program consisted of sending out photos and press releases about his products to the drugstore, mass-market retailing, and chain-store trade publications. As a result of my efforts, stories about his products and/or company appeared in print every month. In addition, I arranged for business trend stories to appear.

With only one salesman to service the entire country, my client was able to make dramatic headway using the tools that I provided him. After stories appeared, I collected reprints of those stories into portfolios which the salesman would leave with the buyers of each chain store he called on. The buyers had already read about the products, and it is obviously easier to sell something someone has read about than something about which they know nothing. The portfolio of articles served to reinforce what the buyers had already read; furthermore, the collections of articles served to impress the buyers with our growing success, and they naturally wanted to boost their own sales and profits by selling my client's products.

In addition, I mailed buyers a one-page letter every month; the letter consisted of brief paragraphs describing how well we were doing, which stores had ordered our products, and facts about the increasing market for our thirty foot-care products. The combination of monthly trade publicity and direct mail pieces reaped the kinds of rewards we were all working to accomplish: In three years, my client reached his goal of success.

The owner of the company subsequently sold the mail order side of his business for a substantial sum. While the retail business continues to operate profitably, my client has now exercised his option to pursue another dream: he designs and builds luxury double-hull sailboats that sell for about $145,000. Once he has turned that business into another successful enterprise, he will undoubtedly turn another of his dreams into a successful reality.

Private Eyes: By generating a regular barrage of publicity, I was able to make Check-a-Mate Investigations of New York City the most successful premarital and marital investigation service in the United States!

Within four months of getting Check-a-Mate as a client, I got its principals on ABC's *20/20*. During that period, I also got them two major stories in *The New York Times*. One appeared in the Sunday edition, the other on the front page of the second section during the week. Within the next few years, they appeared on virtually every daytime television talk show, including *Oprah, Donahue, Maury, Geraldo, Jenny, Montel*, etc. They were also seen on prime-time television, including *Larry King Live, Dateline NBC, Eye to Eye with Connie Chung, Prime Time, A Current Affair, Hard Copy,* and more. Dozens and dozens of magazines and newspapers also did stories, and Check-a-Mate became more successful than any of us had anticipated.

I next suggested that they begin to license others to open Check-a-Mate offices in various parts of the country. I sent a press release to *Business Week,* which ran a story entitled "When Prince Charming Has A Rap Sheet." A subsequent tidal wave of inquiries from retired police officers flooded Check-a-Mate's phone lines.

The business continues to be a cash cow, for infidelity never takes a vacation.

Designing Women: Through my efforts, I helped two women get a million-dollar-plus interior design commission!

In 1990, two creative women contacted me because they wanted to make the commercial world a more attractive place while also making a decent living for themselves. One cold winter morning, I met them for coffee at a diner in New York's midtown. They told me what they wanted to accomplish, as well as their individual stories. One had been a dance therapist, the other a buyer in the garment business. They had left their respective careers, having suffered proverbial burn-out. They simultaneously went to work for a commercial interior design company where they became friends. After a year, they agreed that even without formal design training, they could open their own commercial interior design company. Having incorporated a business, they utilized their contacts and were able to get some small showroom clients in the Empire State Building and a few other buildings. They designed showrooms and offices for a handbag company, a costume jewelry company, a lingerie company, and a few shoe companies.

After meeting with them and learning their goals, I put together a marketing and public relations program for them. A month later, articles and ads that I had created began appearing in print. I sent reprints of those articles and ads to a specific list of real estate lawyers in New York City. One of those lawyers recommended my clients to a client of his, China's largest manufacturer of exported shoes.

My client was signed to remodel and design a luxurious office and showroom building that the Chinese company had purchased on a fashionable Manhattan street. The shoe company had earmarked $1.25 million for the interior design project!

Six months after getting that commission, my client completed the project, and I arranged for several stories about their work to be published. I made reprints of those stories, and mailed each one along with a brochure and covering letter to several hundred shoe companies. As a result, my client got three additional shoe clients, each of whom required large, new showrooms and offices. Not bad for two women who had no formal training as interior designers!

Incidentally, when the absence of certain skills became an obstacle to their carrying out projects, they simply hired others to execute the appropriate tasks. Even so, they shared a sense of color, design, and proportion that was both exquisite and superbly intuitive.

Teaching Success: How one classroom suggestion led to $300,000 of orders in just two hours! This inspiring example of success is taken from my college-level course, "How To Market and Promote Your Small Business." I mention it because you are a student of this book, and I hope you will enjoy the kinds of success that many of my students have enjoyed.

One of my students had been a New York City high-school art teacher for twenty-five years. He had retired and decided to pursue a second career as a designer of attractive and intelligently crafted presentation cases for photographers and architects. He brought several samples to class one evening, and we were all impressed. I suggested he take several of those samples to a photographic trade show at the Javits Center, not as an exhibitor, but as someone who could show others his handiwork.

He returned to class the following week, and we were all eager to hear what had happened.

"I showed my cases to several exhibitors. Two of them, European camera manufacturers, placed orders for $300,000 worth of cases. They plan to use the cases as premium incentives."

The entire class rose and gave him a round of applause. He had, after all, made more money in just two hours than during his last five years of teaching! Hopefully, this book can give you ideas on how to increase *your* business!

POWER PROMOTING

CHAPTER 1

Identifying Your Market

It's extremely difficult, if not impossible, to sell air-conditioners at the North Pole, to sell diet books to people who can't get enough to eat, to sell parachutes to submarine sailors, or to sell electric heating blankets to nomadic tribes in subtropical deserts. Obviously, one must choose appropriate markets for one's products/services.

If your promotions are to result in increased sales and profits for your business, you must identify both conventional and unconventional markets. This chapter will demonstrate, by example and prescription, how to identify those markets that are likely targets for your promotional efforts.

I hope that each of the following examples gives you food for thought, for you too can find new and effective ways to market your products and services, using creativity instead of large sums of money.

Obviously, it is essential that you identify not only existing markets, but also new markets that no one has yet thought to go after.

One need only look around to see how other companies have found new markets for their products: telephones in cars; advertising atop taxicabs; video screens on airplane seats; and vans that provide more personalized transportation to busy commuters than do public bus services, for example. Some of those van companies have also branched out to provide traveling psychotherapists, haircutters, manicurists, and personal exercise trainers.

Here are more examples:

1. If you have a catering service, you may be able to expand it by providing services to housebound consumers.
2. If you own or lease a taxi that has down time, you may be able to generate additional business by transporting pets to veterinarians and kennels.
3. If you are a cosmetologist, you may not only provide makeup tips at department store counters or apply makeup to local television guests, but you may also provide personalized service to those who are housebound. People in particular need of such services might be those undergoing the discomforts of chemotherapy treatments, for example.

In other words, wherever there are gatherings of human beings, there are possibilities for providing services and/or products. The examples of ways to extend markets that follow should provide you with some helpful ideas.

DISCOVERING HIDDEN OPPORTUNITIES FOR YOUR BUSINESS

In the Introduction to this book, I wrote about a private detective agency that became my client in early 1990. When I first met with the principals of Hill Street Security & Investigations, I learned that the company's primary field of endeavor was to provide guards for EPA Super Fund Clean-Up sites as well as for fast food chains and industrial properties. However, since the company was listed in the yellow pages under Investigators, it received numerous phone calls from women who wanted to find out if their boyfriends, fiancés, or husbands were unfaithful. We decided that premarital and marital investigations could be the source for a successful business. We subsequently formed a subsidiary called Check-a-Mate, and test-marketed it by taking out four consecutive ads in the classified section of *New York Magazine*. The results were nothing short of phenomenal.

After that, we decided that there were unusual cases that would generate a considerable amount of publicity. On a regular basis, I wrote and disseminated press releases with such headlines as "Adultery On The Rise," "Short Men Cheat More than Tall Men," "The AIDS Police," "Check-a-Mate Angels Nail Cheating Spouses," "80-Year-Old Casanova," "This Hon For Hire," and many more. Exhibits 1-1, 1-2, and 1-3 show some of those press releases. The result was not only major stories in such daily newspapers as *The New York Times*, *Daily News*, and *New York Post*, but stories on many major television programs as well. The *New York Times*, for example, ran a story that stated, "There arrived a press release with a most alarming headline: 'Adultery on the Rise.' It said two private detectives who operate a business called Check-a-Mate, calculate that spousal cheating, even in this age of AIDS, is increasing. Specifically, by 5 to 10 percent a year." Exhibit 1-4 shows the article that appeared in the *Daily News*.

Check-a-Mate was also the subject of stories on *20/20*, *Eye to Eye*, *Dateline NBC*, *Hard Copy*, *A Current Affair*, and others. The principals of Check-a-Mate appeared as guests on *Oprah*, *Donahue*, *Maury*, *Jenny*, *Geraldo*, *Montel*, and *Larry King Live*.

Within a year after contacting me, Check-a-Mate had become the premier detective agency specializing in marital and premarital investigations.

We had not merely identified a new market, we had dominated it. As a result, many Check-a-Mate copycats sprang up, and some of

EXHIBIT 1-1 Press releases are a good way to generate publicity. Here is an example of a press release publicizing Check-A-Mate Investigations.

From: Jeffrey Sussman, Inc.
        Marketing Public Relations
        249 East 48 Street
        New York, N.Y. 10017

For: Check-a-Mate, a division of
       Hill Street Security & Investigations

Contact: Jeffrey Sussman
           (212) 421-4475

FOR IMMEDIATE RELEASE

CHECK-A-MATE ANGELS

NAIL CHEATING SPOUSES

New York, N.Y. – Two years ago, the Check-a-Mate private detective agency began using women as decoys to learn if their clients' husbands or boyfriends would be unfaithful. It has proven to be such a succesful device, one that hundreds of women have requested, that Check-a-Mate has hired six beautiful female operatives. They are known as the Check-a-Mate Angels, and they are experts at looking gorgeous while performing the roles of undercover detectives.

Upon the request of clients, the Angels put themselves in places where errant husbands and boyfriends go to meet women. While wearing audio tape recorders and sexy outfits, the Angels may chat with someone's husband or boyfriend, but they never lead them on, never entrap anyone. They are simply there, and if someone comes on to them, they respond in a friendly but noncommittal way.

"I started using female decoys because a number of my female clients requested that I do so," stated Jerry Palace, who owns

4

EXHIBIT 1-1 (continued)

Check-a-Mate. "It's an easy and efficient way to learn if your husband or boyfriend is looking for someone with whom he can have an affair."

"I had one recent case that is typical of many of my decoy cases," said Jerry Palace. "A woman was engaged to a high-powered investment banker. He would go skiing by himself in Aspen on weekends, go sailing in the Caribbean with friends, travel around the world looking for investment opportunities, visiting friends in Paris, Milan, Rio, and other fashionable cities. He never took his fiancée, who has her own career as a lawyer. She is also an heiress; in time, she will inherit millions of dollars. He considered himself a ladies' man, the kind of guy who believes that women find him irresistible. He enjoys using his power and wealth, being the center of attention, and getting others to do his bidding. Before my client would actually marry him, she wanted to test his fidelity, so I sent one of our Angels out to Aspen, where she met him on the slopes. He asked her to join him for lunch. Rather than returning to the slopes after lunch, he suggested they go to his bedroom for another kind of athletics. In fact, he said he wanted to 'ski her slopes.' My Angel taped it all, and it was presented to the client. She decided to break off her engagement and look for a man whom she could depend on."

"Such cases have become commonplace," noted Mr. Palace, "because people do not want to be betrayed, do not want to go through the pain and trauma of divorce. They want some reassurance that they are not about to make a painful mistake."

In the last month, the Check-a-Mate Angels have handled more than two dozen such cases. In about a third of the cases, the client was correct in being suspicious.

EXHIBIT 1-2 It's a good idea to give your press release a catchy headline. This release is titled "80-Year-Old Casanova."

From: Jeffrey Sussman Inc.
       Marketing Public Relations
       249 East 48 Street
       New York, N.Y. 10017

For: Check-a-Mate, a division of
      Hill Street Security & Investigations

Contact: Jeffrey Sussman
          (212) 421-4475

FOR IMMEDIATE RELEASE

80-YEAR-OLD CASANOVA

New York, N.Y. – The detectives of Check-a-Mate are invariably asked to investigate the adulterous affairs of people aged 21 to 55. The subjects under investigation may or may not be married; however, none of them have ever been senior citizens. Then, one day last week, Jerry Palace, a former New York City detective and owner of Check-a-Mate, got a phone call from an angry and suspicious woman.

"She had been dating a man for ten years," said Mr. Palace, "and felt that he was seeing another woman." Such calls are not unusual for Check-a-Mate, but it had never before gotten such a request from a woman in her mid-seventies. "She wanted us to follow her boyfriend, a man in his mid-eighties!" exclaimed Mr. Palace. "She was convinced that he was (to use her words) 'fooling around with a young floozy in her sixties.' So we followed him for several days, and he turned out to be even worse than his girlfriend had suspected: he had two other girlfriends, both in their sixties. He would visit one in the morning, the other in the afternoon, then have dinner with his steady of ten years. All

EXHIBIT 1-2 (continued)

I can say is that this guy was really getting the most out of his retirement."

"I finally told the client that I had videotaped and photographic evidence that her boyfriend was indeed being unfaithful. I also suggested that viewing the evidence might make her feel even worse than she already did."

"Never mind," she said. "Show me. I'm a big girl."

"Well, I presented her with the evidence, and she sure got mad. She even threw an ashtray against her kitchen wall. She then lit a cigarette and thanked me. I didn't know what she was going to do; then after several days, she called to say that she had confronted him. He broke down and told her he really loved her, but was frightened of growing old; seeing other women made him feel like a young man again. When faced with the prospect of losing the woman he loved, he promised to break off the other relationships and to remain faithful.

"The client sent a check with a note saying my services had been worth every penny. She could finally stop feeling angry and suspicious. She and her boyfriend are now in Florida where they plan to buy a condominium."

EXHIBIT 1-3 Another press release with a captivating headline.

From: Jeffrey Sussman Inc.
Marketing Public Relations
249 East 48 Street
New York, N.Y. 10017

For: Check-a-Mate, a division of
Hill Street Security & Investigations

Contact: Jeffrey Sussman
(212) 421-4475

<u>FOR IMMEDIATE RELEASE</u>

<u>ADULTERY ON THE RISE</u>

New York, N.Y. – While most people have assumed that adultery has become less common as a result of AIDS and other sexually transmitted diseases, two private detectives have evidence that they believe proves that adultery has been increasing by between 5% and 10% per year.

"We look into the backgrounds of about 2,000 individuals each year," said Mr. Palace, "and our records indicate that the number of people committing adultery has increased rather than diminished over the last four years. In the early and mid-eighties, people were fearful of catching AIDS and so curbed their behavior. However, the people who are going to cheat on their spouses generally believe that 'safe-sex' practices will ultimately protect them. Most of them use condoms and/or spermicides that kill viruses, and hope they will be protected. Almost carefree, they pursue their sexual inclinations."

Jerry Palace operates Check-a-Mate, an investigation service that looks into the behavior of errant husbands and wives as well as into the backgrounds of the prospective spouses of those who do not want to marry someone with a criminal background or

8

EXHIBIT 1-3 (continued)

whose lifestyle may portend a marriage that will fail. Typical cases include a young investment banker whose prospective spouse claimed to have been a model and an aspiring actress; in fact, she had been a prostitute for an escort service. One young woman's father hired Check-a-Mate to investigate her boyfriend, and the detectives subsequently learned that he led a bisexual life. He later developed AIDS. A divorced mother of two small children hired Check-a-Mate because she was considering marrying a man who had recently moved to New York from Los Angeles; he turned out to have a criminal record for child molestation.

Check-a-Mate, located in New York City, is a division of Hill Street Security & Investigations, a company involved in all aspects of investigations as well as in providing security for politicians and other celebrities.

---

them even had the temerity to use my client's trademarked name! A lawyer was hired who promptly put an end to such violations.

Going A Step Further

Next, I decided that the business was so well known that we could successfully license the use of the name to qualified investigators in other sections of the country. I sent out a press release announcing that Check-a-Mate was the first private detective agency specializing in marital and premarital investigations to open licensed offices around the country. About ten days later, *Business Week* ran a story entitled "When Prince Charming Has a Rap Sheet." From that day forward, retired police officers and other professional investigators called to buy Check-a-Mate licenses. Another market had been identified and turned into a profit center!

THIS HON FOR HIRE

A decoy makes private eyes at suspicious lovers

By LENORE SKENAZY

ATTENTION, ALL TWO-timing bums: BEWARE. That luscious bit of loveliness who just walked into your office — the one who looks like the apple did to Adam — is she really available? Or is she perhaps a wriggling bit of bait, hired by your suspicious beloved?

These days, you never know. Engaging private decoys to test a lover's loyalty "may not be the fairest thing," admits private eye Gerry Palace, "but it's a trend."

As co-owner of the Check-A-Mate investigation firm in Manhattan, former NYPD detective Palace usually provides clients with routine surveillance work — background checks, husband-trailing, the snapping of incriminating photos. But lately several women have been requesting a more ... *proactive* approach: Why wait till sweetie finds a woman on his own? Send in the bait!

Tabitha S is the gal on the hook.

"I love doing this," says the thirtysomething Westchester secretary turned part-time decoy. Although she has never been an actress, Tabitha (not her real name — she's undercover) takes to her roles with rare zeal. "You make sure you look really nice the day you go in there," she says. "And then you have to be outgoing, but not brassy."

While her job is not to come on to the mark, she certainly plays along. She giggles. She nods. She wears a wire.

Laura D. — not *her* real name either; she's a client — hired Tabitha through Check-A-Mate to check out her boyfriend, George, a hairdresser. Laura and George had been dating for half a year, and were talking about moving in together. "But you know when your antenna goes up and you feel something's not right?" asks Laura. "There was just *something*. It seemed to me like he would come on to people, he would flirt with my friends and I thought, 'If he does this in my presence, what does he do when I'm *not* there?"

She found Check-A-Mate through an ad. "I said I'm not

'His mouth went open, and his first response was, "You have no right to do this!" '

at a point where I want to waste any time." Send in a decoy.

Tabitha went in for a haircut.

"I asked him about different styles, told him I wanted my hair a different way, I looked at magazines with him. And then he started flirting with me." She told him the cut was just wonderful. She promised to come back in a week for a rinse.

"The second time, he got into my personal life. 'Are you single?' Of course, I said I was." That much was true. " 'What do you like to do?' I told him in the winter I ski, in the summer I go to the beach, go bike riding, and one thing kind of led to another. Then

he said, 'Would you like to go out for dinner?'

"I wanted to kill him. Here he has a girlfriend and he's cheating on her. But it's like really *I'm* getting *him*. It's a great feeling."

On the date, Tabitha was wearing a wire when George suggested, "Now I think it's time we get to know each other better. Do you have your own apartment?"

Sorry, she said, she had to get up early the next day. She never saw George again.

Laura did. "It was better than sex," she laughs. "I asked him what he did on Wednesday night, and he said he worked late and he was so tired and he got takeout Chinese food and he was surprised I didn't call, he would've loved to talk to me. And I said, 'You're amazing. I cannot believe you're lying to me; you think I'm stupid.' " And with that, she whipped out a little Toshiba tape-recorder and pressed play.

"Well, his mouth went open, and his first response was, 'You have no right to do this!' And then he said, '*How* did you do this?' "

"We charge $50 an hour," says Palace.

"The best $600 I ever spent," says Laura.

TABITHA CAN'T WAIT for her next assignment. Though most of her detective work involves simply trailing people — "No one ever suspects women of being private investigators" — it's the decoy work that turns her on.

On the one hand, she's the bait. On the other hand, she's the one with the reel. "It's like, hey, I got another one!"

Fry him up.

(Lenore Skenazy is a frequent contributor to The Gazette.)

DESIGNING WOMEN BECOME SHOWROOM EXPERTS

In 1990, two women contacted me. They wanted to promote and market their commercial interior design firm. Since they were neophytes who would be competing with companies that had been in business for decades, we decided they should concentrate on areas about which they had some knowledge. Since one of the women had worked in the garment center, we decided that showroom designs offered a promising opportunity; most other interior design firms prefer decorating offices, which are far more plentiful than showrooms.

I did some research into the frequency of showroom designs and the correlation between new designs and increased business. I wrote an article, under my clients' by-lines, about the positive correlation and created a print ad for the *New York Real Estate Journal*. After the article and ad appeared, I ordered reprints, wrote a solicitation letter, and bought a list of approximately 750 real estate lawyers— new showroom tenants typically have their lawyers negotiate their leases, and ask them about other services. Several weeks after sending out the solicitation letter and reprints, a lawyer who represented a major shoe manufacturer responded. He arranged for my client to meet with his client. Prior to that meeting, I created a four-color brochure, a slide presentation, and a script for my client to follow during their presentation. They competed against two other companies; one had been in business for 25 years, the other for 18. My client was hungry and ambitious; the others regarded the opportunity as nothing out of the ordinary. My client got the job, for which the shoe company had earmarked $1.25 million. I promoted the work they did for the shoe company, writing articles and ads. Again, I made reprints and wrote a solicitation letter. The result was that my client was signed to do three additional shoe showrooms! They had become experts in the field of decorating showrooms, not just for shoes, but also for accessories and clothing.

11

TAX CHEATS MAY BE A MARKET: AN UNUSUAL NICHE OVERLOOKED BY THE COMPETITION

Here is another example of targeting a special market: An accountant with a successful Florida practice had become highly experienced in negotiating unpaid and unfiled taxes with the IRS. It was done under a program called "Compliance 2000, Offers In Compromise." There were few, if any, accountants doing such work in New York City. I created an ad for him which appeared in *Crain's New York Business*, a weekly publication. All those who responded to the ad were in the real estate business, which had gone into a depression that caused once successful brokers and building managers to lose much of their income. With little income, they had nothing left over to pay their taxes. Based upon the response to our ad, I wrote an article entitled "How To Negotiate Unpaid, Unfiled Taxes." It ran, along with the ad, in the *New York Real Estate Journal*. The response was nearly overwhelming. He acquired so many clients from the real estate business that he had to hire an assistant! I also followed up that publicity with stories in financial magazines and daily newspapers.

I learned next that many people who had not paid their taxes had liens placed against their real property. While one cannot get a list of such tax liens in New York City, that information can be obtained easily in Westchester and Nassau counties, which lie just beyond the borders of New York City. We sent someone out to the county clerks' offices, where we could get as many names as we could record. I composed a letter explaining what my client could do to help, and that the cost was relatively modest. While most direct mail pieces get a 1% to 3% response, we were averaging between 10% and 15% each week! It took a mere six months to make that accountancy practice successful. And it was done simply by identifying specific markets, then targeting those markets with the most direct and cost-effective approaches.

BROADEN YOUR MARKET BEYOND THE OBVIOUS

Prior to opening to my own company, I worked for a mid-sized public relations, advertising, and marketing company. In 1984, I had been recommended to the publisher of *The World Almanac & Book of Facts*. At that time, *The Almanac* had been published for 105 years and had never been on the *New York Times* bestseller list.

Each year, *The Almanac* runs a contest for junior high school students throughout the United States. It is called the Heroes of Young America. Every year, a movie star or a rock-and-roll singer takes first place. The ensuing publicity is nice, but it doesn't cause a dramatic increase in sales. I decided to promote other winners on the list who would have a special appeal to formerly untapped markets.

In 1984, there were three unusual names on the list of heroes: President Reagan, Pope John Paul II, and Katharine Hepburn. There had never been a president and pope on earlier lists, and there had never been a female movie star of Ms. Hepburn's age. Since 1984 was an election year, I contacted the White House press office and told them that President Reagan had been chosen as a Hero of Young America. I further told them that we wanted to present him with a plaque in the White House, take a photo of it, and distribute it with a press release to every newspaper, magazine, and radio and television news program in the country. It would not only be beneficial to *The World Almanac*, but it would help the president during the upcoming election. The White House agreed, and the publisher and I took off for Washington, where the presentation was made in the Roosevelt Room of the White House. The photo (shown in Exhibit 1-5) and press release appeared in more than 1,200 newspapers!

Next, I contacted the press secretary for the Catholic Archdiocese of New York. I explained that the pope had been chosen a Hero of

EXHIBIT 1-5 Finding a celebrity that is somehow connected to your product can be helpful in promoting that product. Here, a celebrity photo with President Reagan (receiving an award from Jane Dystel, editor of *The World Almanac*) is used to boost sales of *The World Almanac*.

Young America. Since we could not afford to fly to the Vatican to present a plaque to the pope, we requested permission to present it to then-Archbishop O'Connor, whom we had read would soon be making a trip to the Vatican. The Archbishop's press secretary agreed, and the presentation was made in the Catholic Center in New York City. A photo of the presentation (shown in Exhibit 1-6) and a press release were sent not only to the Catholic News Service, but to every Catholic publication in the country, including those published by Catholic high schools, colleges, and universities. The response was phenomenal. There are thirty million Catholics in the United States, and we may have gotten one-tenth of them to buy *The Almanac*!

Though Katharine Hepburn did not feel up to posing for a photograph, we sent her a plaque naming her a Hero of Young America. Thereafter, I sent a press release to virtually every women's magazine in the United States, many of which ran our story with their own photos of Ms. Hepburn.

By extending the market for *The World Almanac* beyond those who worshipped at the shrine of Michael Jackson (that year's number one hero), I had been instrumental not only in getting *The World Almanac* on the bestseller list of *The New York Times*, but in making it number one on the list! Indeed, so successful was the approach that *The Times* even wrote a story about *The Almanac* reaching number one on the bestseller list for its first and only time in 105 years!

To keep the momentum going, I created a four-page newsletter that I sent to every retailer who carried *The World Almanac*. I told the retailers about all of our wonderful and effective promotions. I further explained that the promotions would create an enormous audience for *The Almanac*. As a result, the retailers ordered many more copies than they had in previous years, and they tended to sell out their entire stock.

EXHIBIT 1-6 Another celebrity photo (in this case it is Jeffrey Sussman and Jane Dystel with Archbishop O'Connor) used to promote *The World Almanac*. This photo ran in many Catholic publications.

16

REACHING BUYERS WHO ARE NOT IN STORES

In the late 1980s, a food inventor had created a delicious new ice-cream product called "Love Bites." It consisted of premium vanilla ice-cream covered with Godiva-quality chocolate. It was delicious! However, because shelf space for frozen foods is precious and expensive, and is generally controlled by large food companies who make special deals with supermarkets, my client could not get any conventional shelf space. He could not reach shoppers in stores. We decided, instead, to reach a market of pedestrians. To reach that perambulating market that didn't head off with shopping lists in its pockets, we rented approximately 400 ice-cream carts that could be wheeled onto the streets of New York. Rather than targeting a market that would come to us, we would go onto the streets and attract an outdoor market. How to attract that market without spending a fortune on advertising became a singularly important priority.

I went to a local radio station and made a deal with them: on each ice cream cart, we would put a transistor radio that would be tuned to the station. The radio station announced every hour that passersby should stop by and pick up an entry blank for a contest that would award a number of special prizes, including a week at Club Med, a 25% discount on a new car, stereo equipment, free dinners at great Manhattan restaurants, and much more. I had gotten the vendors to donate products or services in exchange for free air-time, and Love Bites was mentioned every hour for several weeks. At the end of the promotion, the company had achieved its goals. Other than a monthly fee to my company and the cost of renting the carts, it had been able to keep its expenses to a bare minimum and reach a different market from that normally found in stores.

A RECESSION-PROOF MARKET

In 1971, I owned a gymnastics and exercise school in New York City. While we enrolled many children of the wealthy, we also had many children from lower-middle- and middle-class families. Any significant downturn in the economy would result in those parents withdrawing their children from extracurricular activities.

So that my business would not suffer as a result of periodic recessions, I decided to open a gymnastics camp in a wealthy community. I chose the Hamptons on the eastern end of Long Island. It is a playground for millionaires, who readily spend large sums on their children without batting an eye. To rent a facility that would provide all the necessary minimum accommodations for a gymnastics camp would cost at least $10,000 for two months, not including additional expenses for salaries, insurance, and advertising. I had no desire to put my capital at risk.

I looked around for a situation where I could trade my services for the appropriate real estate. I learned that a number of investors had purchased a beach and tennis club in Bridgehampton. The club comprised fourteen acres, two swimming pools, ten tennis courts, an enormous clubhouse, and several thousand feet of beachfront property. The club would naturally be crowded on weekends, but during the week, mothers and children would be the only ones using the club's facilities. I believed that if the club could offer gymnastics, swimming lessons, sports, arts & crafts, and drama to youngsters, it would have a marketing tool for dramatically increasing its adult enrollment: mothers could play tennis and swim while their children learned gymnastics and became physically fit.

I wrote a proposal to the owners in which I suggested that I would pay the club 15% of my gross in exchange for using the club Monday through Thursday, from 9:00 A.M. to 4:00 P.M., for a period of eight weeks. After several meetings, the owners agreed; and for five years, I operated a highly profitable gymnastics and sports camp that had cost me no up-front cash. Indeed, there was no way I could have afforded to rent a beach and tennis club for eight weeks in the Hamptons. It would have cost several hundred thousand dollars to rent such a club!

Of course, once I made a deal with the owners, I aggressively marketed and promoted the camp. I not only attracted the offspring of many famous actors, singers, business leaders, and politicians who spend their summers in the Hamptons, but I promoted that fact to others who wanted to have their children associate with the children of famous people. In addition, I got more children to pass the President's Council on Physical Fitness and Sports test than any other camp in the Hamptons. I was able to set up a photo opportunity with the President's Council, and I received a Presidential Sports Award for my accomplishments. I further publicized all of this, and it worked to generate even greater enrollment in my camp.

That experience taught me that one can look for new markets not just for the sake of business expansion, but also to avoid the vicissitudes of an often-fickle economy.

THE COMPETITION MAY BE UNDERESTIMATING THEIR MARKET

There is an enormous consumer appetite for sports memorabilia products. The market continues to grow, and is kept at a high pitch of excitement during televised sports. Many entrepreneurs have capitalized on that market; too many of them, however, have introduced cheap, poorly made products. In some cases, they may enjoy great success because no one has introduced superior and affordable products.

Several years ago, two men who worked in the printing business decided to manufacture a model of Yankee Stadium. There were other models available, but none were as dramatic, detailed, interesting, and impressive as the one my client had created. They had hired a paper architect and graphic designer to create an architecturally accurate model. In fact, the model was completely accurate, down to the advertising on the outfield walls.

It was obviously a product that, if brought to the attention of discerning sports fans, would enjoy enormous success. I determined that there was nothing else on the market as thoughtfully and impressively created as my client's model. I had identified the market for the product, but I still had to figure out a means for letting baseball fans know of its existence and superior quality.

At the time that we wanted to introduce the model, George Steinbrenner had begun talking about moving the Yankees out of New York City. I had also learned that the Yankees do not own Yankee Stadium, New York City does; and the stadium comes under the care of the New York City Parks & Recreation Department. I decided that we would give a portion of our profits to the Parks Department, so that we could contribute to the upgrading and maintenance of Yankee Stadium. In effect, my client would be helping New York City to keep the Yankees in Yankee Stadium. Next, I decided that we would give "pre-built" models of the stadium to radio and television personalities who had contributed, by word or deed, to keeping the Yankees in New York. I booked my client on numerous radio and television programs, where they not only awarded the model of Yankee Stadium to the hosts of the programs, but where they also had an opportunity to state their toll-free number numerous times. It worked time and time again. Their phone lines kept ringing, and they sold thousands of models at $24.95 each. In fact, the model was so popular that my client was able to raise the retail price to $29.95, and the Stadium still enjoyed brisk sales!

MARKET EXPANSION

Having gotten that far, I next wanted to expand the existing market. I contacted more than a dozen mail-order catalogues that sell games, toys, and sports-related items that are deemed unique and fascinating. I sent out copies of models, press kits that I had written, photos, and comments of praise that I had elicited from celebrities. After several months, I was able to get a catalogue company called Bits & Pieces to accept models for a test market. The test proved successful, and the catalogue ordered many more models. I also made contact with retailers, and got them to stock and sell the model as well. Altogether, the venture proved extremely successful.

Of course, it helped that the product was uniquely well conceived and, in its final form, handsomely crafted and meticulously detailed. Indeed, anyone who purchased the model was pleased with it, and many felt it was so attractive that it could be hung on a wall as a work of art. It became apparent that if there is a market for a product, and the quality of available products is not very high, there is a significant opportunity for superior products to dominate that market.

Ralph Waldo Emerson, that clever old American marketer, is alleged to have stated, "If a man can make a better mousetrap than his neighbor, though he builds his house in the woods, the world will make a beaten path to his door."

NEW LAWS CREATE NEW MARKETS FOR COMMONPLACE PRODUCTS

A man who creates and installs signs was suffering from diminished sales and profits. There were too many competitors, providing cheap, unimaginative signs. Each one was offering the same products; each one was underselling the other. He contacted me, asking that I help him expand his market.

There are few items as commonplace as signs: Exit signs, elevator signs, handicapped-parking signs, telephone signs, etc. Boring, yes, but absolutely required by law.

Rather than go after the usual market of landlords and building managers, I decided that my client needed to segment the market, and sell his signmaking capacity to different customers.

Hotels and hospitals, obviously, need signs. In addition, hotels, hospitals, and all other public buildings must be in compliance with the Americans with Disabilities Act (ADA). I read the Act and learned what signs are required by hotels and hospitals, two large consumers of signs. I then wrote two articles, under my client's by-line, about how hotels and hospitals must be in compliance with ADA and what kinds of signs they must exhibit. The two articles appeared in trade publications read by hotel managers and hospital administrators. When the articles were published, reprints were made. Each reprint was mailed with a covering solicitation letter to a list of hotel managers and hospital administrators. I had purchased the list from a company that compiles and then sells lists. Ten days after the direct mail pieces had been sent via bulk rate from the post office, a trained telemarketer, working from a script, called each person who had received a direct mail package. Appointments were made for my client, and deals were closed.

I next realized that traditional and/or landmark buildings also require signs that are in compliance with ADA regulations. I wrote another article, again under my client's by-line, and arranged for that to be published in a magazine that is read by the owners and managers of traditional buildings. The magazine printed my client's name, address, and telephone number, inviting its readers to contact him. My efforts resulted in a considerable amount of new business, much of which turned into repeat business.

I had succeeded by turning my signmaking client into an unusual artisan who understood the demands of the ADA law as well as the needs of customers. He was also able to create signs in virtually any style, whether for modern hospitals or historic churches. In addition, he could create signs in every language known to mankind, and he did so. Indeed, some of his Chinese signs contained beautiful calligraphy that attained levels of artistic elegance.

STAY FLEXIBLE:
ADAPT TO CHANGING MARKETS

It is essential that one remain flexible in order to remain competitive. It is not enough to undersell one's competition or to offer a greater product line. One must know how to reach out to existing markets *and* how to extend one's reach to new markets. Furthermore, one must be able to alter the image and purpose of one's company as the marketplace alters.

Nearly a century ago, stables in New York City became parking garages, coal distributors became oil distributors, fan manufacturers began to make air-conditioners, adding-machine companies switched to calculators, horse-drawn carriages were replaced with cars and trucks. The following stories illustrate some other examples of how savvy entrepreneurs have changed their businesses to adapt to new markets.

From Dresses To Jeans

In the 1960s, I knew someone who had a dress manufacturing company; he manufactured low-end dresses for other companies. He was a subcontractor. He had his finger on public tastes; and when he saw that jeans were rapidly becoming a fashion craze, he began manufacturing jeans. He even opened several retail outlets that sold only jeans. He went from making a comfortable living to being a millionaire!

From Horses To Trucks

I knew a man in Chicago whose grandfather owned and operated several horse-drawn milk-delivery carts; his son took that company and built it into one of the country's major trucking companies.

From Food To Dancing

The history of entrepreneurship consists of people who could change the identity and purpose of their businesses with the ease and precision of chameleons.

When I was a college student in New York City, for example, I used to eat lunch in an old barnlike structure in the East Village, near New York University. It was cheap, dark, had sawdust on the floor, thick candles on the tables, and was highly atmospheric. In the late sixties, the disco craze arrived in New York like a hurricane. The owner of the restaurant (which I frequented for its delicious Greek salads) had decided that there was a lot more money in running a disco. With a minimum of renovation and even less redesigning, he opened an exceedingly popular disco that attracted people from all over the city. He used to arrive at his restaurant driving an old VW bug; when he became a disco king, he had money to burn and arrived in an elegant silver Jaguar. He was no longer a failed painter who ran a restaurant to earn a living; he was a disco entrepreneur, a star of the night who took away each day's earnings in a pair of laundry bags!

START A BUSINESS TO MEET A NEW MARKET NEED

Before concluding this chapter, I shall give you one more example of someone who created a business for a new marketplace and then successfully expanded it.

When I opened my gymnastics camp in the Hamptons, I needed a bus service to transport those campers whose parents could not deliver their offspring to camp. I contacted a local school bus company, but it was closed for the summer. The owner was not interested in recommissioning his vehicles.

I subsequently met a young man who had been in the advertising business in New York. He had grown tired of city pressures, and decided to leave the chaos and turmoil of the city for the comparative tranquillity of the country. He didn't have a driver's license, and there was no public transportation in the Hamptons. He purchased a van, hired someone to drive it, and offered transportation not only to those who had no cars and no licenses, but also to the disabled, and to children and pets. There were also thousands of people who spent the summers in the Hamptons, but otherwise worked in New York. They often needed things shipped in and out of the city. The young transportation entrepreneur soon had a fast-growing and popular delivery business. It seemed that anything that could fit on a seat was transported on what became the Hampton Jitney.

I remember once putting six or seven of my campers on the Jitney service and being surprised to see a German shepherd and a golden retriever sitting on two front seats. They sat impassively, looking straight ahead and bothering no one. On another occasion, I saw a large potted plant strapped onto a seat, apparently being shipped from someone's New York apartment to their beach house.

Because traffic to and from the Hamptons on Friday and Sunday nights is extremely congested, many people do not want to drive their own cars. The transportation visionary saw a large potential market of people who would rather be driven than drive. The Hampton Jitney bought several large buses and began transporting those people in the utmost comfort. In addition, the Jitney served soft drinks, snacks, and provided newspapers and magazines. The buses stop at various central locations in the city, each one convenient to the hundreds of thousands of people who spend their weekends in the Hamptons. The Jitneys have proven so popular that they run daily, all year round. Indeed it has proven to be so popular that it now has competition!

QUICK TIPS FOR SUCCESS

As long as one keeps exploring new possibilities and is willing to take risks, one can successfully go into a new business, or expand an existing business. All it takes is drive, imagination, persistence, intelligence, and an understanding of how your products/services fit into a specific market.

If you already have a business, I suggest that you do an extensive investigation of who might be representative of new markets. If, however, you are thinking of opening a new business, you should not only investigate how large the conventional market is for your products/services, but should also investigate whether there exists a market that none of your competitors is tapping into.

Remember that your own interests, skills, and talents should not only determine what kind of business you operate, but should be used to help you explore new markets.

If you love to cook, you might become a caterer and cook for those who cannot cook for themselves. If you love sports, you might create products for others who also love sports. If you love animals, you might provide a service or products for pet owners. The sky is the limit. You need only exercise your imagination. In dreams begin reality.

CHAPTER 2

Your Name In Lights: The Media Can Make You Famous

The media (which includes all sorts of newspapers and magazines, as well as radio and television) can be used to create interest in your products and services. Before you can go to the media, however, you must understand the media's needs, and how you can meet those needs. The media has a voracious appetite for stories, but those stories must have an appeal that will get the attention of their audience. In effect, you must go to the media and say, "I have a story that your audience will find irresistible, informative, helpful, beneficial, and that they just can't live without."

Now that you've gotten the attention of a reporter or editor, you had better be able to deliver a package that has more to it than beautiful wrapping.

A FORMULA FOR SUCCESS FROM AN EDITOR ON HIGH

Shortly after I graduated from college, I applied for a job as a night copyeditor with one of New York's tabloids. During the course of my interview with an old, grizzled editor who looked as if he could have been cast in *The Front Page*, he asked me if I knew the four essential ingredients for a story in his paper. Before I could answer, he stated: "Pets and vets, kids and [here he used a vulgar expression for a woman's breasts]. You want a story in the paper, you better have, at least, one of those items. You get all four, plus a good photo, and you might even land on the front page!"

Of course, it is not as simple as that makes it sound, and many newspapers are too lofty to condescend to such an editorial formula. Nevertheless, look at television news stories and commercials: many of them use sex, pets, and kids to sell products and to get your attention. Since we are no longer a warrior nation, war vets rarely get the kind of attention that was once commonplace; the patriotic aura has become dim indeed. However, twists on the vet story are still useful, hence gays in the military were a hot subject, as were women in combat.

CREATING PRESS RELEASES THAT REACH OUT AND GRAB ATTENTION

Now that your focus has narrowed to four essentials for getting publicity, you should know how to construct a simple press release that will get attention. Keep in mind that if a dog bites a man, it is not news; however, if a man bites a dog, it's probably news. So not only do you have to focus on some elemental item to get attention, you should also create a story that turns logic inside out.

All press releases, no matter how outrageous, must still answer six basic questions: Who? What? Where? When? Why? and How? These questions should, if possible, be answered in the first paragraph. When one looks at a finished press release, or a published news story, one should see that it is shaped like an inverted pyramid. Most of the information will be at the top of the story. As one reads down, a story will have less and less important information, so that one should not need to finish reading it to get all the pertinent facts. Newspapers as well as television news shows have limited space and time. A newspaper, for example, may have only five inches of one column for a story. If it cuts the remainder of the story, the story must still make sense and be complete, hence the need for all essential facts to be up front. Similarly, a television newscast may be able to give your story only 30 seconds. If the essential facts are not in those 30 seconds, but come after 45 seconds, your story will be incomplete and of questionable value.

A STORY FOR SUPERMARKET TABLOIDS

Let me give you an example of a story that I wrote for Check-a-Mate, the private detective agency. The agency had recently investigated a man who was cheating on his wife. The man was a compulsive philanderer, and he was a mere 5'4" in his stocking feet. None of that is newsworthy. However, the following headline made it newsworthy: SHORT MEN CHEAT MORE THAN TALL MEN! On the first page, I wrote that short men cheat more often than tall men, because they can sneak around and not be seen as readily as tall men. Jockeys, therefore, tend to cheat more than basketball players.

The story ran in several supermarket tabloids and resulted in hundreds of phone calls from women who were married to short men! I had not said anything that wasn't true, I had merely reversed a popular prejudice that tall men are more attractive and sexual than short men; the man-bites-dog approach. Furthermore, I had added a note of humor to the piece by implying that such behavior portended a previously unreported trend. Newspapers generally report trends if the trend has social, economic, or political ramifications. In addition, you should know that certain stories are appropriate for one kind of newspaper and not for another. For example, my "short men" story would not have been appropriate for The New York Times, but it was ideal for supermarket tabloids. One must also get only that kind of publicity that will produce increased business; otherwise, the publicity only serves to massage one's ego.

Exhibit 2-1 is a press release that is an example of the format in which a press release should be written.

EXHIBIT 2-1 Press releases should follow a basic format; here, basic questions like Who? What? and Why? are answered in the first two paragraphs.

From: Jeffrey Sussman, Inc.
        Marketing Public Relations
        249 East 48 Street
        New York, N.Y. 10017

For: Check-a-Mate, a division of
       Hill Street Security & Investigations

Contact: Jeffrey Sussman
           (212) 421-4475

FOR IMMEDIATE RELEASE

SHORT MEN CHEAT

MORE OFTEN THAN TALL MEN

New York, N.Y. – Does one's height have anything to do with faithfulness and adultery? According to Jerry Palace, owner of Check-a-Mate, a private detective agency that investigates spouses and prospective spouses, "the greatest number of cheating spouses whom I have investigated are short men, ones who are five-feet-five or under."

Asked what accounted for this, Palace said: "I have asked a number of spouses, whom I have investigated, if they felt their shortness had anything to do with their cheating. One man, no larger than a jockey, said that he felt he could sneak around and few people would notice him. And another man, about five-feet-four, told me he had always felt insecure because he was so short. He felt that the only way he could prove his virility was to commit adultery over and over again. He had been married four times and throughout each of his marriages he committed adultery on a regular basis; he is being divorced by his present wife, who is one of my clients."

EXHIBIT 2-1 (continued)

But don't tall men cheat too? "Of course," stated Palace, "I followed one semiprofessional basketball player whose wife had asked us to keep tabs on him. When I caught him in flagrante delicto, he said he knew he would get caught: 'I'm just too tall to get away with this. I can't hide,' he complained."

Palace said, "about 65% of the men I find cheating are short; some are real short, no bigger than seventh graders."

Jerry Palace, before opening Check-a-Mate, a division of Hill Street Security & Investigations, had been a highly decorated New York City detective, who made hundreds of arrests and received many awards and commendations. "It's a lot safer following adulterous husbands or lovers, whether they are tall or short, than it is chasing muggers and murderers," confessed Palace. "There have been men who wanted to beat me up. And the toughest one was a little welterweight fighter. I just got out of his way and lived to work another day."

GETTING YOUR FOOT IN THE PUBLICITY DOOR

Here is an example of a publicity event that was introduced with a press release. There are countless beauty contests every year. There are swimsuit contests, wet t-shirt contests, bikini contests, nude beauty contests, etc. While those contests all satisfy one of the four elements I listed, none of them has an inherent man-bites-dog component.

I had a client who manufactured and distributed thirty different foot-care products. I wanted to create awareness of his products without resorting to expensive advertising.

What is the funniest part of the human anatomy? Could it be appendages that no one would consider beautiful? That's right, it's the feet. Of course, there is an exception to every rule, and foot fetishists, I'm sure, would go crazy for a nicely shaped foot or a plump big toe.

I was not, however, out to appeal to such specialists. Instead, I wanted to get the attention of those people who would regard a "Most Beautiful Feet" contest as oddly amusing. I sent out a press release announcing that such a contest would be held in a hotel ball-room in New York City. The winner would receive a one-year foot modeling contract: her tootsies would appear on all the company's boxes and on in-store posters. More than 400 women showed up for the contest! Not only was it covered by local newspapers and various magazines, but *CNN* covered it, and the subsequent story ran every hour for 24 hours. My client got an enormous amount of publicity that resulted in a significant increase in the sales of his products.

The press release that I sent out was headlined: SHY WOMEN TO SHOW OFF THEIR BEAUTIFUL FEET. Not only are feet not the subject of beauty contests, but shy women do not appear naked in public. I had taken a mundane subject and arranged it so that it had become newsworthy. Exhibit 2-2 features that press release, and Exhibit 2-3 shows an article in one of the magazines that picked up the story.

Choosing The Right Media For Your Story

Having written a provocative press release, one that can attract potential customers to your business, it is essential that you locate the ideal medium for your story. The two press releases cited above would not have been appropriate for *The Wall Street Journal* and *The New York Times*. One proved ideal for the *Star*, the other for *CNN* and the *Daily News*.

In order to determine which publications or television programs might be appropriate for your product/service, you must determine where and how you can reach your customers. If, for instance, you want to reach people in the real estate business, then a real estate

EXHIBIT 2-2   Another press release with an engaging title.

From: Jeffrey Sussman Inc.
         Marketing Public Relations
         249 East 48 Street
         New York, N.Y. 10017

For: Professional Foot Care Products

Contact: Jeffrey Sussman
            (212) 421-4475

FOR IMMEDIATE RELEASE

SHY WOMEN TO SHOW OFF THEIR BEAUTIFUL FEET

New York, N.Y. – Many women have dreamed of being models. Some may be extremely pretty, even beautiful, but do not have the precise kind of looks that can lead to a modeling career. Many more, who are also quite attractive, are simply too shy to exhibit themselves to the scrutiny of a camera lens. As one such woman said: "Posing in front of a camera makes me feel as if I'm being observed under a magnifying glass."

In response to an advertisement that Professional Foot Care Products placed in a New York City newspaper inviting women to participate in the Second Annual Most Beautiful Feet Contest, the company received hundreds of phone calls from women who want to enter the contest but have always been too shy to enter any kind of beauty contest. Some of them had thought of entering beauty contests before and had even made initial inquiries about doing so, but then felt they could not go through with it. Some said they were urged to do so by their parents, boyfriends, or husbands. Ultimately, however, the women felt that such kinds of contests would prove humiliating, or they felt that their shyness would only make them uncomfortable and unhappy.

EXHIBIT 2-2 (continued)

"Many of the women who called to inquire about our Beautiful Feet Contest," said Dr. Leonard Feldman, president and CEO of Professional Foot Care Products, "said that our contest offered them an opportunity to show off their feet to a panel of judges and not experience butterflies in their stomachs, weak knees, or sweaty palms. One woman even said: 'this may be a break-through opportunity for me, liberating me so that I can perhaps not feel so self-conscious about my body.' Such feelings seem to be those of many of the women who will be entering the contest on October 22."

"In fact," continued Dr. Feldman, "the winner of the contest will get a one-year modeling contract that will mean her feet will appear in newspaper and magazine advertisements, on posters in drug stores, and in television commercials. Not bad for someone who is shy."

The Second Most Beautiful Feet Contest will be held at the Algonquin Hotel on October 22 beginning at noon.

---

publication would be appropriate. If you wanted to reach the buyers at the large mass-market retailing chains, then you would send your story to a publication such as *Mass Market Retailing*, which is read by buyers.

When I undertook to help Professional Foot Care Products get into retail outlets, I wrote stories every month that were sent to at least a dozen such publications. Often the stories were "new product stories," which introduced buyers to new products that they should carry on their shelves. The stories were always accompanied by an 8 × 10 glossy, black-and-white photograph, so that buyers could see how attractively the product was packaged. Only little children, incidentally, are told not to judge a book by its cover; in the real world, marketers always judge products by appearances,

EXHIBIT 2-3 Once again, the press release leads to effective promotion. This story (and many others like it) was printed in a magazine after an initial press release was issued.

Beautiful feet contest held

NEW YORK—Leonard Feldman, president and chief executive officer of Professional Foot Care Products Inc., was among the judges who chose the winner of the Most Beautiful Feet Contest, held at Manhattan's Algonquin Hotel recently.

The winner, Jenna Ward, seen behind Feldman, has been signed to a foot-modeling contract to promote Professional Foot Care's products. Ward will take part in what Feldman says is a major marketing effort with nearly $500,000 that is earmarked for a nationwide advertising campaign.

just as people often make a first judgment of others based upon appearances. It is the reason why manufacturers spend so much time developing the most eye-catching and appealing packages for products that might otherwise seem mundane, boring, vapid, or trivial. Indeed, the entire automobile industry is based upon selling cars that are sleek, sexy status symbols.

When I promoted the Most Beautiful Feet contest, I made sure that the drugstore and mass-market retailing publications received press releases and photos, because I wanted the buyers, who were also our customers, to know how much time and effort we put into promoting our products to customers. That, in turn, would cause them to increase the size of their orders.

BRINGING HOME THE BACON FOR YOUR PUBLICITY: DIRECTORIES

After you decide who the potential audience for your product/service is, you must make a list of publications which those consumers regularly read. There are general newspapers and magazines; and there are special-interest publications, known as "trade" publications. You can find a list of such publications in two reference books, *Bacon's Newspapers* and *Bacon's Magazines*, which are published in Chicago. These books cost several hundred dollars to purchase, so you may want to see if your library possesses current copies.

Each of the *Bacon's* books lists newspapers by state and city, then lists the names of editors who cover particular topic areas. Magazines are listed according to topic, from accountancy to zoology. Editors are listed at their levels of importance and authority.

You may occasionally want to reach varying levels of consumers. For instance, Professional Foot Care Products wanted to reach buyers at drugstores and mass-market retailers, but it also wanted to reach end-users, which it did via the publicity it obtained from its Beautiful Feet contest. By reaching the end-user, the consumer, it could increase demand for its products, thus getting buyers to increase the quantity of their orders. When new or increased orders were placed, I would write stories about that fact for the trade publications, which would then cause other buyers to place new orders or to increase existing orders.

SIGNS OF NEWS; NEWS OF SIGNS

In Chapter 1, I told the story of my campaign for a signmaker. Crucial to that campaign was a story that I wrote, under his by-line, for the *New York Real Estate Journal*. The *Journal* is a biweekly trade newspaper read by the owners and managers of commercial real estate in New York City. Of course, prior to writing the article,

I had spoken with the publisher to make sure that he would be interested in publishing an article on the topic I had proposed.

The article's appearance resulted in numerous phone calls from interested customers. As good as that was, it was not enough, so I purchased a list of New York building owners and managers from a professional list company. I wrote a solicitation letter on my client's letterhead (see Exhibit 2-4) and mailed it with a reprint of the article to all those on our list.

EXHIBIT 2-4   An example of a solicitation letter.

Dear Building Owner/Manager:

Here is an article that I believe you will find of interest and value. It was written for the New York Real Estate Journal and deals with the Americans with Disabilities Act and the responsibility of land-lords and building managers in having all appropriate signage. Indeed, without such signage, there is no way that one can be in compliance with the law. Yet, by having the appropriate signage, you will not only avoid fines, but you will also significantly reduce your liability from negligence should a tenant be injured in your building.

Our company is one of the oldest sign companies in the United States, and has created signs for some of the best known build-ings in New York City as well as in many other cities.

We have created everything from illuminated canopies to new signs for lobbies, elevators, and hallways. As a result of the Amer-icans with Disabilities Act, we have also created thousands of signs that have a braille component.

We have developed an unsurpassed reputation for competitive prices, reliable and timely service, and attention to detail that makes many of our signs unique creations.

(continued)

EXHIBIT 2-4 (continued)

While most signmakers and designers merely do one or two drawings prior to creating a new sign, we begin each job by performing a site survey that determines what kinds of signs are needed and how many; then we prepare a detailed written proposal, including costs; finally, we create samples of signs, so that our clients can see and feel. By using models of signs, we permit our clients to make intelligent decisions, altering a color here, changing a line there. The result is not only satisfied customers, but also signs that handsomely serve the specific purposes of landlords and building managers.

If you would like to know more about how our signs can help you maintain compliance with local and federal rules and regulations, please contact me at your convenience. I look forward to hearing from you and showing you how we can be of service to you.

Cordially,

Ten business days later, I had someone in his office, working from a telemarketing script that I had written, phone each person who had received our direct mail package. The result was far more business than came in from the publication of the article alone.

Such a procedure is often referred to as "selling the sizzle." In other words, you should always attempt to sell your own publicity, to generate even greater sales than occurred from the first round of publicity. (Chapter 3 will deal with this process in detail). Those phone calls, by the way, generated an enormous number of appointments for my client to sit down and directly sell to his potential customers. He had done more than merely get his foot in the door, he got himself and his products into a decision-maker's office. In many cases, that was as good as making the sale.

The Media Plus More

In the case of the signmaker, a story in a particular publication, though helpful, would have been insufficient to get him all the business he required. When choosing the appropriate medium or media for your publicity, therefore, always keep in mind that the publicity must generate sales, and it may be essential to use your publicity as a marketing tool by putting it into direct mail solicitations.

MAKING THE ENVIRONMENT PAY OFF

Another client of mine was a woman who performed Phase I and Phase II assessments on buildings. In case you have never heard of a Phase I or II, it is merely a way of determining if a building contains asbestos. The presence of asbestos is a red flag to banks and insurance companies that lend money to purchase buildings or to refinance mortgages. If a building contains asbestos, it may cost more to rid the building of the asbestos than the building is worth! No lender, after all, wants to repossess a building that is not worth the money that was lent to pay for it. In addition, no buyer wants to buy a building that contains asbestos, because he may be unable to sell it.

I had written an article for my client, entitled: "Only A Gambler Would Purchase a Building Without an Environmental Assessment." The article appeared in building, real estate, insurance, and banking publications, since those were the publications read by people who could hire her or recommend her to others. After the article's appearance, I purchased a list of mortgage bankers, mortgage brokers, insurance company executives who lend money, and building owners and managers. As in the previous example, I purchased the list from a professional list company. Thereafter, I wrote a solicitation letter and mailed it, with reprints of the article, to each person on the list. Bankers received an article from a banking publication, insurance executives received one from an insurance publication, mortgage brokers received one from a mortgage publication, and building owners and managers received one from a real estate publication. Ten days later, I had a college student call each of the recipients and set up appointments for my client. The student worked from a telemarketing script that I had written and wrote down all responses. The results included my client being put on recommended lists by banks and insurance companies, and ultimately being hired to do assessments of stores, gas stations, factories, hospitals, a military base, and dozens of office and apartment buildings. (Be sure to read the next chapter so that you, too, can learn to "sell your sizzle.") I cannot emphasize too often that the right media may also include direct mail and telemarketing, for each is a highly focused medium that can generate substantial sales for your business. And each must be considered when making a list of possible media outlets for your publicity.

ONE GREAT PRESS RELEASE CAN CAUSE A STORM OF MEDIA ATTENTION

In some cases, a provocative press release, without any additional efforts on your part, can generate an ongoing wave of marketing-oriented publicity that is like a snowball rolling down a hill, becoming larger and larger, more and more imposing with every revolution. It not only generates several initial stories, but those stories generate even more stories, and those stories generate other stories, and the subject not only has a life of its own, but it grows like a monster.

For example, after Check-a-Mate hired a beautiful model to visit a store owned by the husband of one of its clients who suspected him of being unfaithful, the *Daily News* did a story about it. The decoy-model who visited the store looked beautiful and sexy. She did not begin a conversation with the husband and carefully avoided flirting with him once he started talking to her. In other words, she did everything possible to avoid entrapping him. She simply gave the appearance of being a beautiful customer. The husband, however, made a pass at her, asked her out for a drink and dinner.

She nonchalantly accepted the invitation and secretly recorded his proposition to have sex. She then departed. After the *Daily News* story appeared, a syndicated columnist called Check-a-Mate, interviewed Jerry Palace, and published a story that appeared all around the country. Within weeks, Oprah Winfrey decided to devote a show to the topic. The female client (wearing a wig and sunglasses), her husband (also in disguise, of course), the model (looking more beautiful than usual), and the detective all appeared for an hour.

A few of the questions from Oprah and the audience were unsettling, but everyone was prepared for the worst. They answered all questions intelligently and tactfully. The audience loved it, and so did the millions of viewers at home: Check-a-Mate's phone rang off the hook for several weeks thereafter, with thousands and thousands of phone calls from wives and unmarried women who suspected their husbands and fiancés of cheating. Check-a-Mate had to put in several additional phone lines to handle the enormous volume of calls.

HOW TO PREPARE FOR A MEDIA INTERVIEW

Most clients, in contrast, are unprepared to deal with the potential snares of media interviews, and must be rehearsed—just as presidential candidates are rehearsed to debate their opponents. The last thing you want is to sound unprepared, ignorant, or foolish. All the potential good that can result from a positive media interview will go down the drain if you do not know what you are doing. Indeed, if you appear ignorant or foolish, you can undermine your credibility and authority, and it is often impossible to regain it.

One thing I always tell clients is not to lie. In the world of media creations, you can destroy yourself in an instant if you lie. If you don't know the answer to something, it's much better to tell an interviewer that you don't know. You should say that you will be happy to get the information and report back to them. They will appreciate your honesty and effort.

In order to prepare yourself for a media interview, you should make up a list of potential questions that you would like to be asked as well as those you may expect to be asked. The questions will usually be based upon a press release or letter that you have sent to media outlets. Once you have composed the questions, then you should rehearse answers with a sense of confidence. Your answers should be clear, informative, and to the point. If you are asked an embarrassing question, never say "no comment." Such a response invariably implies a motive to hide something that is bad. Instead, have a reasonable explanation ready.

There are some very successful interviewees who seem to care little about the questions they are asked; they have their own agenda and will adeptly change the subject by speaking interestingly about a topic that is important to them. If you do so on live television or radio, your words will be heard instantaneously. If, however, you try the same thing with a print reporter or if your words are being taped for a later broadcast, you better make sure that what you have to say is more interesting than the questions being asked and that you are saying things that are of genuine interest to the reporter.

I have seen hapless people bumble and stumble through interviews, getting absolutely no marketing or publicity value from the media. Indeed, I have seen a doctor and a lawyer, who are presumed to be experts in their chosen fields, sound little more intelligent than complete nincompoops. After such a performance, what will happen to their practices? Yet, those individuals were more than merely competent, they were experts in their respective fields. So expert, in fact, that they assumed their expertise would automatically be translated through the media to a grateful public. Neither the doctor nor the lawyer had taken the time or made the effort to prepare a list of questions. And they certainly had not reviewed or rehearsed any possible answers.

If you have done something about which the media will condemn you or one of your products has not lived up to its claims, the worst thing you can do is to behave like an old-fashioned gangster, pulling your coat over your head or hiding behind a newspaper, usually one that has headlined your imminent demise. Instead, you must behave like a successful politician, offering helpful and credible explanations that will help to restore a reputation under attack.

This has, indeed, become an important art form, employed not only by defense lawyers representing celebrity criminals, but also by large corporations whose products have been tampered with, or companies whose products were shoddily manufactured and resulted in terrible injuries for consumers. I'm not passing a moral judgment on any of this; I'm merely reporting what is happening, with the hope that the knowledge ultimately benefits you as well.

It is unusual for people to find themselves in such circumstances; however, since this book deals with all aspects of marketing and promotion, you should know how to deal with all eventualities.

QUICK TIPS FOR SUCCESS

If you are going to use the media to generate publicity for your business, you must learn to write an effective and provocative press release, one that tells a story of value that others will want to read or hear.

In addition, you must carefully choose the media outlets for your press releases; your choices should be based on reaching those people who are in a position of increasing your sales and profits.

On certain occasions, such publicity should be further marketed to potential customers through direct mail followed by telemarketing.

If your publicity will result in media interviews, you should prepare yourself for such events by making lists of questions and rehearsing thoughtful responses.

CHAPTER 3

Selling The Sizzle: How To Use Publicity To Increase Sales and Profits

Publicity should not exist with borders around it. If it is more than the superficial fluff associated with celebrities, publicity must have an organic life that permits it to grow into new forms and to have far-ranging results. Countless products and experts throughout the land were born out of unique and successful public relations programs that had specific marketing goals.

While many kinds of publicity have the power to generate increased sales and profits, others require the beneficiary to market that publicity so that it continues to generate additional business. Whether reformatted as brochures, newsletters, or direct mail pieces, print publicity can be given such an enduring quality that it can be utilized year after year—not only to generate new business, but also to reconfirm professional credibility and authority.

In other words, never let your publicity die gracefully; use it to generate *more* publicity, and more business. Whether in print, on audio tapes from radio interviews, or on video tapes from television programs, that publicity can be used again and again to accomplish a wide variety of marketing goals.

USING PUBLICITY TO LAUNCH AND MAINTAIN A HIGH-PROFILE CAREER

For more than 15 years I have represented an important attorney who is indisputably a leader in his field. I arranged for him to be profiled in *The Wall Street Journal* at about the time that I began to represent him. With their permission, I made a reprint of that story and mailed it with a solicitation letter to the presidents and CEOs of the 500 largest companies in the United States. The solicitation letter went out on the lawyer's stationary and was signed by the managing partner of his firm. As a result of that initial mailing, my client got five of those companies as clients over the next few years.

Now, when prospective clients contact him, he not only sends each of them a copy of *The Wall Street Journal* article, but also reprints of various other stories that I have gotten him over the years. This collection of articles and interviews makes an impressive package, which does a far better job of selling my client than any professional salesperson could do. A salesperson, after all, has an obvious interest in making a sale; articles in prestigious publications, on the other hand, ostensibly are not written to sell their subject. Yet such articles provide explicit and implicit editorial endorsements, which have a cumulative value that is inestimable.

While the lawyer's publicity creates an ongoing image of credibility and authority (that happens to be founded on fact), there are other uses of publicity which are more specific.

FROM MAIL ORDER TO RETAIL SALES: A CASE STUDY

Professional Foot Care Products was the country's foremost remedy foot-care company, selling its approximately thirty products via mail order throughout the United States. When the company hired me in 1990, it had made a strategic decision that it wanted to become as successful in the retail business as it was in the mail order business.

The company had recently hired a dynamite national sales manager, who single-handedly covered the entire country, traveling more than 50% of the year. In certain geographical areas he was able to call upon the assistance of independent sales reps; otherwise, he was the company's magic bullet.

To help him, I began by writing a press release that described how the retail foot-care market was growing, and how large the potential market could be: every person with feet was a potential customer, and there were many chronic foot problems (such as bunions, nail fungus, ingrown toenails, bruised heels, etc.). I explained that Professional Foot Care Products manufactured and distributed a sufficient variety of products to address most of these problems (of course, the company made no representation to deal with problems that only doctors could treat). The press release also distinguished Professional Foot Care Products from its competition by noting that its products were created not primarily for comfort, but rather to effect remedies. Finally, I stressed that all of the products were impulse items that required little or no advertising. People suffering from particular problems would go into a drugstore, see the products on a rack, and purchase those products that would remedy their problems. The suggested retail prices of the products were sufficiently modest that few consumers would think twice about making a purchase.

In short order, stories began to appear in the appropriate trade publications (such as *Mass Market Retailing*, *Chain Drug Review*, *Drug Store News*, and other similar publications). Exhibits 3-1 and 3-2 show two of the articles that appeared. In addition, new product stories about each of the thirty-odd products began to appear on a monthly basis. Each story featured a photo of the new products, and retailers were invited to call and order the products for their stores.

EXHIBIT 3-1 Because of a press release about Professional Foot Care Products, stories began to appear in various trade publications. This article appeared in *Chain Drug Review.*

REPRINTED FROM:

Chain Drug Review
Reporter for the   Chain Drug Store Industry

Vol. 12, No. 23   Published biweekly, every other Monday, monthly in May and December by Racher Press Inc. $2 a copy   August 27, 1990

Chain Drug Review/August 27, 1990

Mail-order foot care firm makes switch to retailing format

NEW YORK—The entry of Professional Foot Care Products Inc. into the retail market will double the multimillion-dollar private company's sales and quadruple revenues this year, according to president and chief executive officer Leonard Feldman. "It's a smash hit in chain after chain," Feldman says of the introduction of Professional Foot Care's line into retail outlets after 18 years of mail-order distribution only. The line of such products as heel cushions, arch insoles and bunion cushions has been accepted or is being tested in such chains as Pay Less NW, SuperRx Drugs Corp., Peoples Drug Stores, Drug Emporium Inc., K mart Corp., Woolworth Corp. and McCrory Corp.

The company's sales are exceeding those of Dr. Scholl's products on a per-square-foot basis, Feldman claims, noting that the two companies occupy different niches of the foot care market. While Dr. Scholl's offers mainly insoles and corn pads, Professional Foot Care occupies the remedy end of the category.

The line is marketed in stores with a 15- by 14-inch display board with a catalog presentation of color pictures showing the products' applications to different problems. The packaging of the products, which are merchandised on 28-inch-wide racks, carries the same information.

The line is made up of the 16 best-selling products from the mail-order business, so that each one does about equally well. "We've distilled it down so that all we have are winners," Feldman says.

Antifungal liquid

But the fastest-selling item has been Proclearz, an antifungal liquid retailing for $4.99 to $6.99.

Vice president of sales and marketing John Vayianos says the market for Proclearz has expanded from the over-45 population to virtually all people who wear running shoes and sneakers, as well as to women who use artificial nails. "As of now, our figures show that more than 20 million people annually suffer from varying degrees of nail fungus," he says. "And our product is considerably cheaper than other similar products, which sell for as much as $12 to $14."

Feldman calls the company's retail entry "the first exciting thing" in foot care in 50 years. He says Professional Foot Care, which opened a second plant in Cleveland last year, should pass the $100 million sales mark worldwide by 1995.

PROFESSIONAL® FOOT CARE PRODUCTS   A division of PROfessional PROduct Research Co. Inc.
74 20th Street, Brooklyn, NY 11232
PHONE: (718) 768-7383 • FAX: (718) 768-7151

Foot care category undergoes growth

CDR Roundup—The foot care category is expanding, as companies devoted to mail-order and physician supplies businesses break out into the retail arena. And, prescription lines are being broadened and brought over the counter to provide customers and retailers with a more diversified mix. One company that has entered retail outlets is Footsply Inc., based in Armonk, N.Y. The 106-year-old company manufactured foot care products for physicians before entering the chain drug market with 35 items. The company's Pedifix line, promoted as "the podiatrist's choice," includes such items as toe straighteners and separators, arch supports and heel cushions, which it says more than double retailers' average foot care transactions. Footsply says that retailers average $2 per foot care sale while Pedifix product sales average $5.36.

"We are a niche product player," notes Footsply president Chris Case. "Our line has succeeded in chain after chain because we've introduced unique, high-quality products, not those that duplicate other manufacturers'."

The line is available in more than 15 chains—among them, Osco Drug and Big B Inc.

Push sales up

Both Case and Leonard Feldman, president and chief executive officer of Professional Foot Care Products Inc., attribute much of the category growth (averaging from 8% to 11% annually over the past six years) to the growing elderly population. As people enter their 40s and 50s, they are increasingly susceptible to physiological changes resulting in foot problems. This and the increased awareness of self-help remedies have pushed sales up.

Professional Foot Care, which calls itself the largest mail-order foot care manufacturer, sells more than 30 products—among them heel cushions, arch and cushion insoles and donut heel pads. After a three-year study, the company ventured into the retail market, beginning in 1990.

To increase customer awareness of the products, the company has allocated 20% of its annual net profits for advertising and promotion.

In addition, Professional Foot Care products are being sold in such countries as Japan, the United Arab Emirates, Canada and Costa Rica.

"By 1995," says Feldman, "we expect our worldwide sales to exceed $100 million annually."

Schering-Plough Corp., which has had products in the retail segment for years, is the maker of Tinactin, the No. 1 antifungal agent for athlete's foot.

The company is currently promoting Lotramin AF—an athlete's foot product that was formerly available only by prescription but is now sold over the counter.

In addition, the company will release a version specifically for jock itch. Both the original and new product will be supported by a variety of rebates ranging from $1 to $3, bonus packs and ads in such magazines as *Newsweek* and *Time*.

Also, in its Dr. Scholl's group, the company will have rebates and coupon offers for its Back Guard, Hidden Comfort and Smooth Touch podiatric shoe inserts and cushions. Bonus packs with free products will also be available for these items, which will be supported by magazine ads.

The company's odor-absorbing Sneaker Snuffer will be offered to retailers in a bonus pack containing a free foot powder or spray. Support will come from full-page ads in *Sports Illustrated* and the *Sporting News* featuring basketball great Julius Erving.

Interest in the category is also being maintained with wholly new products. Footsply's fastest-selling Pedifix item is PumpPals, a medically designed insole for women's shoes retailing for from $5.99 to $8.99. Over 8 million pairs of PumpPals have been sold in Europe and 1 million pairs in the U.S.

Similarly, Proclearz, an antifungal liquid, is a relatively new product for Professional Foot Care. The company attributes some of the product's success to its $4.99 to $6.99 price, which it says is nearly half that of most competitors. The item is sold nationwide in Kmart Corp. outlets, as well as in drug chains.

49

Buyers who had never heard of Professional Foot Care Products were suddenly reading about the company and its products every month. That certainly opened the door for the company's dynamic salesman; to give him an even stronger hand, however, I had reprints of all published articles assembled into attractive folders. When he called upon buyers of mass market retailing chains, drugstore chains, and superstore chains, he gave each a folder of published articles.

As the salesman signed on retailer after retailer, I publicized his accomplishments to persuade recalcitrant stores that they would not want their competitors to sell products that they didn't have on their own shelves. In effect, his accomplishments provided leverage in inducing other retailers to carry the products.

To maintain a constant level of orders or to increase reorders, I wrote monthly letters to buyers. These letters, which went out on Professional Foot Care's stationery, noted how well the products were selling, mentioned various promotions we had embarked upon to increase sales, invited cross-promotional opportunities, stressed the importance of point-of-purchase displays, and addressed any other topics that would have a positive effect on orders and sales.

I also sold the sizzle to the president of a drugstore chain who had been particularly adamant about not carrying our products. He had refused to take the products, refused to make an appointment with any of us, refused to let his executives talk with us about our products; in fact, he wouldn't even take our phone calls. I wrote to him every few weeks, explaining how rapidly our products were selling. I sent him graphs depicting dramatic increases in sales; I sent him articles about how the foot-care category was growing. He was missing out on a combination of rapid turns, high margins, and customer loyalty. Every time a competitor took one or more of our products, I wrote and told him about it. One thing resistance cannot tolerate is gentle persistence; it's like a water torture where each drop slowly but surely wears down the largest, most indomitable boulder.

He finally capitulated, met with the president of the company and his ace salesman, and agreed to take several of our products. We could not have been happier.

The result of that effort (and, indeed, all our efforts) was that, within three years, Professional Foot Care had gotten its products into virtually every mass-market retailing chain, drugstore chain, and superstore—not only in the United States, but in seven other countries as well. In fact, Professional Foot Care was able to get 15% of the Japanese foot-care market, an unusual accomplishment for a mid-size American company!

I publicized the company's Japanese success, and the president of the company marketed that publicity to help get partners in other countries. In other words, each effort led to another accomplishment, which would lead to something else: the snowball just kept rolling, getting larger and picking up speed.

USING PUBLICITY TO AUDITION FOR A LARGER ROLE

Here's another way to use publicity to generate more business. In this case, I used videotaped television appearances to create an audition tape for a series of television programs.

Years ago, when I represented a physical fitness expert, I compiled several of her television appearances from talk shows into a single videotape. I used that tape to sell her to a large communications company, which made a series of videotapes of her for home use and for airing on its national cable network. Rather than getting paid for single appearances, which had been her previous experience, she was able to get a comprehensive contract that gave her remuneration for on-air shows as well as royalties for in-store retail sales. (I wrote the series of exercise tapes, and so received a credit as a television writer, which I was able to use to get other television assignments).

SUCCESS BY ASSOCIATION

Sometimes, one need not promote oneself beyond the bounds of one's office. Here's an example of a lawyer who used photographs of famous people on his walls to imply how well-connected he was.

Using his business contacts, I was able to arrange for him to be photographed with the President of the United States; he hung that photo in his office. He had photos of himself with a variety of local and national politicians, including senators and congressional representatives. It was all part of building his image: he could successfully represent clients who would have dealings with the government. Indeed, it became a self-fulfilling prophecy: the more he represented clients with the government, the more clients he got. And his selection of photos traced the ascent of his practice.

It is said that an actor's career is nothing more than the collection of roles he has played. Similarly, the public history of a business is based upon a collection of marketing successes, each of which led to the next.

Most of my clients have very down-to-earth goals, and I have used the practice of "selling the sizzle" to help them reach their goals. In other words, the sizzling success documented in their publicity has been sold as an undeniable testimonial.

USING SOLICITATION LETTERS TO SELL THE SIZZLE

A number of years ago, I had a client in the plumbing supply business. He sold a device that could help landlords of commercial buildings save a considerable amount on their heating bills. I arranged for a real estate publication (read by thousands of landlords and building managers) to publish an article by my client, which I had written for him. It explained how the product worked, its efficiency, and its long life span; it further showed how much landlords were spending to heat their buildings, and how much of that cost was wasteful.

After the article appeared, I purchased a list of building owners and managers in Manhattan. I sent the article out with a solicitation letter on my client's stationery. Ten business days later, I had one of my employees make follow-up phone calls. He worked closely from a script, and was able to set up numerous appointments for my client. As a result, my client began to make so many sales, and had so many inquiries about his product, that he had to hire five salespeople to meet the demand. He has continued to use that article for four years without it losing any of its luster, for new customers keep buying his expanded line of products!

Solicitation letters are extremely important, and must reach out and grab the reader in the first paragraph, if not the first sentence. Consumers receive so many direct-mail solicitations that they do not have the time to read each one beyond the first few lines. If their interest is not aroused at the beginning of the letter, post card, or brochure, the missive is quickly crumpled and tossed into the wastebasket—such is the fate of most direct-mail appeals.

In addition, you should know that the rate of positive response to direct mail is only 1% to 3%. So if you are going to go to the effort and expense of direct mail, it had better be as effective as possible!

Exhibits 3-3, 3-4, and 3-5 are examples of solicitation letters that I have sent out on behalf of clients. Each one is about a fairly mundane topic; however, the letters were directed to a targeted group of prospective customers, who would find the content of particular interest. In other words, the letters were not aimed at the general consumer, but at specific categories of consumers who could benefit from the products or services offered by my clients.

If you are unsure about the letter you are writing, show it to people who are members of the category of consumer you are trying to sell. If, for example, you want to sell your products to dog owners, show a few dog owners your letter(s) and evaluate their responses.

EXHIBIT 3-3 Solicitation letters are very important when it comes to getting publicity. The reader's attention must be seized in the first sentence. See Exhibits 3-4 and 3-5 for other attention-grabbing letters.

Dear Chief Engineer/Superintendent:

We can make your job easier, saving you time, effort, and money. Here, for your information, is a copy of an article that I recently wrote. It carefully describes how single cartridge seals can save significant amounts of time, labor, money, and electricity compared to old-fashioned packing and seals for pumps.

We have been installing single cartridge seals in both commercial and residential buildings for years. The response of building owners and operators who have purchased our seal has been overwhelmingly positive. Their savings have been substantial, our cartridge seals are far more durable than old component ones, and our seals are easy to install and maintain.

I urge you to read the attached article, then contact us so that we can explain exactly what we can do for you. We look forward to meeting with you and telling you all about our acclaimed services and products.

Providing solid solutions in sealing technology, there is no other company as responsive and reliable. We are confident that we can prove it to you: Just call us, and we'll get the ball rolling. I look forward to hearing from you.

Cordially,

EXHIBIT 3-4 Targeted solicitation letter #2.

Dear International Business Traveler:

Will your travel agency provide you with a free round-trip limousine service to and from the airport? Will your travel agency give you a $100 rebate on your next international business flight?

EXHIBIT 3-4 (continued)

When you book your first international business flight with XYZ, one of the most sophisticated and experienced travel consultancies in the world, you will receive either a free round-trip limousine service or a $100 rebate on the price of your flight!

We are making this unique offer to introduce you to the finest travel services available. In fact, we believe that once you experience the services of XYZ, you will never want to utilize the services of any other company.

Here are some of the acclaimed services that set XYZ apart from all other travel companies:

- Corporate profit sharing
- Negotiated air-fare contracts
- Upgrades & limos
- Visa & passport services
- Tickets via in-house messengers
- Management reports
- World cash
- Preferred hotel rates

Just one phone call not only gets you all of those services, but it gets you to your destination right on time.

For the best world-wide travel services, the best prices, and the best access to international markets, call XYZ. We will be pleased to tailor a travel program to meet your specific business needs.

Cordially,

EXHIBIT 3-5 Targeted solicitation letter #3.

Dear Hotel Manager/Owner:

Signs are extremely important to the successful function and profitability of all hotels and motels. Signs not only are an effective form of advertising lodgings to customers, but signs are also essential to maintaining compliance with local fire laws, as well as with all the rules and regulations of the Americans with Disabilities Act.

Here is an article that I recently wrote for an important hotel/motel publication.

Our company, one of the oldest sign companies in the United States, has worked on behalf of some of the best-known names in the lodging industry. For example, we have designed, manufactured, and installed signs for XXX as well as for the famed XXX, among others.

Our company has created everything from illuminated canopies to new signs for lobbies, elevators, and hallways. After the Americans with Disabilities Act was passed, we were called upon to create thousands of signs that have a braille component.

Indeed, when it comes to quality, prices, service, and timeliness, no one has a better track record than we do.

While most signmakers and designers do one or two drawings prior to creating a new sign, we begin each job by performing a site survey that determines what kinds of signs are needed and how many; then we prepare a detailed written proposal, including costs; and finally, we create samples of signs, so that our clients can see and feel what an actual sign will look like. By using models of signs, we permit our clients to make intelligent decisions, altering a color here, changing a line there. This results not only in satisfied customers, but also in signs that handsomely serve the specific purposes of the lodging industry.

EXHIBIT 3-5 (continued)

If you would like to know how our signs can help your marketing efforts, and help you to maintain compliance with local and federal rules and regulations, please contact me at your convenience. I look forward to hearing from you and showing you how we can be of service to you.

Cordially,

LETTERS THAT DON'T WORK

Recently, a woman who had opened a dress store contacted me. Her business was dying, and she was desperate to make it successful. She had sent out letters to various groups of women: one letter announced the grand opening of the store; a second letter announced a 20% discount; a third letter told about her wide variety of merchandise. The letters were each about her store, but none of the letters really offered consumers something they could not find at other stores. I told her that she had to offer her prospective customers something more than information about her dress shop and a 20% discount.

"If you're going to have a grand opening, for example, make it truly grand. Have a party. Have refreshments, a band, a fashion show. Give everyone who comes a free, inexpensive gift. In addition, hand each person a series of discount coupons, so that they will be tempted to make purchases. Once you make friends of potential customers, it's a lot easier to sell merchandise to them."

I convinced her to rename the store and start all over again with an opening party. We began by purchasing a list of women who lived within a ten-block radius of the dress shop. Next, we wrote a letter that included all the goodies listed above. The letter was printed on large invitation cards which were inserted into oversized envelopes. Each envelope was addressed by hand.

Our grand opening produced a wonderful turnout, and her store was reborn as a successful dress shop that offered a host of amenities that kept customers coming back.

In addition, we arranged for her to put on fashion shows for women's groups at churches and temples. When members of their congregation purchased dresses at the shows, 20% of the purchase price was rebated to the church or temple. I had shown her how to turn her dress business into a fund-raising device that generated tens of thousands of dollars for churches and temples. Her business took off, and it continues to do well, because my client not only continues to market her dresses in unusual ways, but has extended her market with the help of other women who are taking her dresses and putting on fashion shows in several dozen communities. Each of those women gets a commission on what she sells, as well as free merchandise. All this was done with targeted solicitation letters, offering something that we thought others would find irresistible.

WRITING SOLICITATION LETTERS THAT GET RESULTS

I once worked with a woman who used to come into my office every day and talk about herself. She was very pretty and obviously enjoyed her image. I once asked her if she could talk about something other than herself. She paused for a moment, then said: "Tell me what *you* think of my dress."

That, in a nutshell, is what is wrong with so many solicitation letters. They tell you about themselves, rather than giving consumers an incentive to make a purchase. Writing a solicitation letter is not like writing to your parents and telling them how well you are doing. Your parents certainly care, but strangers do not. You have to put yourself in the shoes of your potential customers or clients, and make a direct appeal to their self-interest. If you do, you'll get a positive response.

Churches and temples, obviously, need to raise money. They do it all the time. They canvass members, asking for contributions; put on parties; arrange trips to the theater; offer gambling nights, etc. So, why not a fashion show where spectators will be encouraged to make purchases? They will want to make such purchases not merely because they all want to own beautiful garments that will make them look attractive, but because they have an interest in helping their religious institution. It's a win–win situation that benefits all involved—and that should be the guiding principle of all solicitation letters.

TESTING RESPONSES BEFORE MAILING LETTERS: FOCUS GROUPS

If you are uncertain about how to approach potential customers, you should put together one or more focus groups. A focus group consists of people who are likely to be members of your customer base. A group of 10 to 20 people is assembled in one room and questioned about services, products, packages, usage, and any other matters that will help you determine how best to market your products/services. In order to test responses to a solicitation letter, prepare two or three letters for the group to read, ask specific questions about the letters, and then ask them to express whatever opinions they may have about the letters. You will learn a great deal, not only about the effectiveness of your letters and what points to include or delete, but also about your products/services.

Of course, focus groups can also be used to determine what kind of packaging will attract the eyes of consumers, the kind of bottle or jar a product should be placed in, the look of an ad, the taste of a food, and the demand for a wide array of services (such as law, accountancy, and medicine). Medical practices, for example, can benefit from focus groups by asking interested consumers what they expect in a waiting room, what kind of behavior they expect from a receptionist or secretary, how the decor of a doctor's office affects them, etc. Obviously, a doctor who follows the results of a focus group will have happier, more relaxed patients than a doctor who makes no effort to accommodate a practice to the needs of patients.

Once you have evaluated the outcome of a focus group, you can decide how to market your products/services in solicitation letters, as well as in your other marketing efforts.

ROLODEX CARDS

While a well-focused solicitation letter can get superb results by itself, there are other ingredients that should be included in most mailings. A Rolodex card is essential. Most such cards, however, merely have names, addresses, and telephone numbers. If people file cards away, they will shortly forget the name of the company that sent the card. Not to be lost in the deck of other cards requires an individual symbol for your business. If you are in the travel business, your Rolodex card might have a picture of an airplane on a tab that can be seen easily. Such an image reminds people of your business even if they have forgotten your name. The image stands out among the letters on the other tabs and announces its purpose.

Some of the images I have created for clients:

1. A leaky pipe for a plumbing supply company.
2. A stethoscope for a doctor.
3. A baby's face for a maker of infant pharmaceutical products.
4. Barbells for a gym.
5. A crossed scissors and comb for a haircutting salon.
6. A diamond engagement ring for a jeweler.
7. The outline of a rose for a florist.
8. A pair of eyes for a contact lens manufacturer.

MAILING LISTS

After you have prepared the solicitation letter (making sure that it aims directly at your prospective customers' interests), and have prepared a Rolodex card, you must purchase a mailing list. Most list companies charge about $65 per 1,000 names, with a minimum order of about $150. Most lists are, in effect, leased: you can use the list once and not again. Many companies place several false names on the list, which will be sent back to the list company. Using such a procedure, they can determine if you are reusing their list. Pressure sensitive labels are easiest to place on envelopes (such labels are also called "peel and stick").

In order to decide what kind of mailing list you should purchase, you must first determine who your potential customers are and where they are located. For example, I did a mailing for a commercial interior design client (described in Chapter 1). I had reasoned that real estate lawyers were in a position to recommend my client to their own clients, especially those who were negotiating leases for new offices or showrooms. I called one of the list companies from whom I regularly buy lists. I had decided that I wanted real estate lawyers in midtown Manhattan, for that is where there is a heavy concentration of offices and showrooms. I provided the list company with zip codes for several midtown neighborhoods. In firms that had many real estate lawyers, I asked for the head of the department or the firm's managing partner. I prepared a separate letter for those lawyers, asking them to post the letter, or distribute copies to their colleagues. I also placed the appropriate number of Rolodex cards in each mailing.

I prepared a mailing to mortgage bankers for another client: I got a list of bankers throughout the entire city as well as several outlying suburbs, for her scope of business extended to all of those areas. For the owner of two espresso bars, I purchased mailing lists of potential customers who lived within ten blocks of each store. I was able to narrow the focus of that mailing list by getting the route numbers used by the letter carriers from the local post office. With that information, the list company supplied me with thousands of names of residents who lived within close proximity of the espresso bars.

After you have procured the appropriate mailing list, you can do the mailing yourself (perhaps with the help of a student whom you can pay by the hour), or you can give your mail package and appropriate letterhead to a mail house. If you choose to use a professional mail house, you will spend considerably more money than if you do the mailing yourself.

If you want to save as much money as possible, you should not only do the mailing yourself, but should get a bulk mail permit from your local post office. You will have to bundle all the mail together, usually by zip code, and deliver it in bulk to the post office. You can incur dramatic savings by getting a bulk mail permit, and I regularly advise my clients to do so.

BROCHURES

In addition to doing mailings of solicitation letters and reprints of articles, it is often a good idea to do subsequent mailings that consist of brochures. Since the first mailing may not get you all the new customers you want, you will need a new device for the next mailing, and brochures are often quite effective. A brochure can be printed in either four colors or two, depending on your budget and on the nature of your business. Obviously, if you own an art gallery or an interior design business, you want to demonstrate the beauty of color, and a black-and-white brochure will hardly do the trick. However, if you are selling industrial equipment (plumbing supplies, electrical fixtures, spark plugs, etc.), you can have quite an effective brochure that uses black-and-white photos only.

You must decide what information should be contained in your brochure. In order to do that, put yourself in the shoes of potential customers. What would they want to know about your company? In most cases, a brochure should contain the following information: a list of products and services, warranties (if any), competitive prices, a few testimonials from satisfied customers, and length of time in business (if you've been in business for a long time—if you've been in business a week or two, keep it under your hat). Make sure you include your address and phone number. If potential customers are not in your local calling area, you should consider getting a toll-free number. Many people will automatically call an 800 number, if given the choice between that and a toll number.

The design of a brochure is extremely important. Even if you have the capacity for desktop publishing, you may not have the eye, sensitivity, and skills of a professional designer. Rather than hiring a high-priced professional, you can often employ the talents of a college student who is studying art and design.

Make sure that your brochure is not printed on cheap paper. A brochure is, in effect, your calling card; and if it says cheap, it will not win you new customers. Most brochures are printed on glossy paper.

You have two choices when mailing a brochure: either it should fit into a #10 envelope (the standard business size), or it should be a self-mailer (in which case one of the panels is left blank, so that you can place an address on it). A self-mailing brochure is simply stapled or taped at one point, stamped, and mailed.

It is also a good idea to include your business card. Simply staple it to one corner of the brochure.

NEWSLETTERS

Another device for reminding customers of who and what you are is a newsletter. I regularly write and design newsletters for many of my clients. If you were to take an $11'' \times 17''$ sheet of paper and fold it in half, you would have the four panels of a conventional newsletter. That is, in turn, folded in thirds so that it is the same size as a #10 envelope. Exhibit 3-6 is an example of a newletter I created for Silver Seagull Environmental Corporation.

EXHIBIT 3-6 Newsletters are a great way to publicize the exact nature of your business. Here is an example of a newsletter created for Silver Seagull Environmental Corporation.

WINTER 1993
$2.00

ENVIRONMENTAL

PUBLISHED BY SILVER SEAGULL PUBLICATIONS • EDITOR: ESTHER SEGAL **UPDATE**

IT'S WORSE THAN ASBESTOS IN THE SCHOOLS!

by Esther Segal

New Yorkers are exposed to asbestos more often than they know; indeed, if they had any idea how often they are regularly exposed, they would rapidly join some back-to-nature movement and flee from yet another threat to their lives.

I have been called upon to do numerous Phase I environmental assessments of buildings that had already been given clean bills of health; many of those buildings were contaminated with asbestos! In addition, there were other hidden problems, such as lead-based paint and poor indoor-air quality that were not addressed in the original environmental report. Why wasn't it reported? Possibly because the previous owners had pressured contractors to give their properties clean bills of health, or contractors may have simply performed slip-shod and sloppy work. It happens more often than people realize.

In addition, I have examined office buildings on behalf of hundreds of new tenants. Many of the landlords of those buildings, while tearing out old installations prior to building new ones, were exposing tenants and contractors to asbestos. Such exposure to environmental hazards is not only injurious to one's health, but those whose health has been impaired by such exposure will sue landlords for millions of dollars.

If those concerned tenants had not contacted me, or someone like me, they would never have known of the presence of carcinogens.

It is essential that people realize that it's not only the schools that are a danger to us and our children: There are many buildings, both private and public, which are just as dangerous, just as potentially injurious.

There are people who know of the problem, but they're saying nothing. The school asbestos problem is the focus of their attention and of the media's attention, but they should be focusing on the overall problem, since asbestos is not isolated to schools, and dangers from environmental hazards are not isolated to asbestos. In fact, many buildings pose a significant health threat to the populace of this city.

Since millions of people are not going to abandon New York, it is essential that the city put together a comprehensive plan to mitigate and eventually eliminate the problem of asbestos. To begin, the governor should appoint an environmental czar, who would function very much as the Consumer Affairs Commissioner functions. The office of an environmental czar should have legal powers to impose fines while ordering landlords to eliminate carcinogens from their buildings. An environmental czar should have the responsibility of integrating state and city rules and regulations into one coherent policy. Furthermore, no governmental entity, such as The Board of Education, should be exempt from the authority of an environmental czar. If we do not act now, and if we continue to let our environmental problems fester, we will see a significant deterioration of health in this city and a corresponding increase in the cost of treating the victims of environmental hazards.

EXHIBIT 3-6 (continued)

ENVIRONMENTAL UPDATE

RACE PLAYS ROLE IN ENVIRONMENTAL CLEAN-UPS

According to a hard-hitting, investigative report in The National Law Journal, the federal government favors white communities over minority ones in its clean-up of hazardous sites as well as in its pursuit of polluters. The legal publication showed that fines were 500% higher near white populations than those near minority populations. This disparity exists solely on the basis of race and income. In addition, abandoned hazardous waste sites in minority areas take 20% longer to be placed on a priority list than areas in white neighborhoods.

Only by increasing funding and testing of all sites will this problem be curtailed and addressed as it should be.

INSURERS MUST DEFEND PROPERTY CLAIMS

The highest court in Illinois ordered seven insurance companies to defend an insulation contracting company in property damage suits resulting from asbestos-containing building products installed by the contractor. The unanimous ruling by the Illinois Supreme Court affirmed an appellate court's decision. Since the contractor's liability had not been determined, the court did not address whether the insurers had a duty to indemnify any damages awarded against the family-owned company. The claims seek to hold the contractor liable for damages caused by sprayed-on asbestos fireproofing materials it installed during the 1960s and 1970s.

The name of the newsletter should reflect the nature of your business. I have created newsletters with the following titles:

1. *Compliance Alert* (for companies that must be in compliance with all OSHA rules and regulations).
2. *Labor Update* (for a labor relations lawyer).
3. *Signs of the Times* (for a sign manufacturer).
4. *Design Views* (for an interior design company).
5. *Nuts and Bolts* (for a tool company).
6. *Play Ball* (for a baseball memorabilia company).
7. *Hot & Cold News* (for an air conditioning and heating company).
8. *VRRRROOOMMMM!* (for an auto mechanic).

Each of the four pages of the newsletter can be divided into two columns. One column on the last page can be left blank, for newsletters should be self-mailers. That blank column gets a mailing label and your return address. One interior column should contain topics that readers may want additional information about. They can clip that column and mail or fax it back to you. It should have your fax number at the top or bottom of the page.

You should be listed as the editor of the newsletter, just below the title. Each story in the newsletter should have a headline, indicating the nature of the story that follows. Stories should be about new industry developments, things that will be of interest to existing or new customers. There should be a column of general advice to consumers. For example, if you are an interior design company, you may want to tell people which colors have the most relaxing effect, which are the most conducive for a productive work environment, which are considered romantic, etc.

You might also publish the results of surveys that you have conducted among a small number of customers. If you own an auto repair shop, your customers may be interested to hear what other people's pet peeves are (or what they most worry about) when getting their cars repaired. They would probably want to know how to tell if a mechanic is honest, or charges too much.

You should also include news about yourself, your staff, and even your family. If you recently installed new equipment, let people know about it. If you received an award, let readers know about that too. If you have a new baby, don't just announce it, run a photo: nearly everyone enjoys a baby photo.

When I worked on *The World Almanac & Book of Facts* campaign, I created a newsletter that was sent to retailers throughout the United States. The newsletter explained not only how we were promoting *The World Almanac*, but what we were doing for the other books the company published. As a result, retailers not only ordered many more copies of *The Almanac* than they had in previous years, but they also ordered copies of other books that *The World Almanac* was publishing for the first time. The newsletter contained a column from the publisher, pictures of celebrities to whom we had presented awards, pictures of the covers of all the books we published, contests, and a trivia quiz. It proved to be an extremely effective marketing tool, one that helped to make *The World Almanac & Book of Facts* number one on bestseller lists across the country.

Newsletters personalize your business, and automatically confer a level of authority and expertise on you. Why would you be writing and mailing a newsletter if you weren't an expert in your field?

Newsletters should typically be printed in one color, on a white background. Navy blue is an excellent color, one that implies confidence and trust. There are some colors, however, that can be closely identified with a category of business. Green, for example, is an excellent color for a gardening or nursery business, or for any business that deals with the outdoors. For a floral business, I suggested a masthead that consisted of red, yellow, and green. In addition, a bouquet of flowers, in those colors, became the company logo and was used at the top of the newsletter. For a law firm, each white sheet of the newsletter was imprinted with light beige pin stripes because it was that kind of "white shoe" firm. For a client, who sold seasonal fruits and vegetables, we had a different color for each of the seasons: pale blue for spring; a bright green for summer; a brilliant, almost luminous orange for the fall; and a silvery white for winter.

For most companies, newsletters are mailed quarterly; however, some are mailed every eight weeks—in particular, newsletters from lawyers and certain accountants, because there is a plethora of new information that they must impart.

Newsletters should go to both existing and prospective customers. You should compile carefully selected mailing lists and keep those lists updated. There are many small printing companies that can design and print your newsletter. Prices will vary, based on the quality of paper, numbers of colors, number of copies, and also the printer's location. It is a good idea to get prices from five to eight printers, some urban, some suburban, and some rural. You should let them know that you will be publishing the newsletter on a regular basis, and would like a special price as a repeat customer.

If, however, you have desktop publishing capacity and a good sense of design, there is no reason why you cannot create your own newsletter. The number of copies that you need will determine whether you should do it yourself or farm it out.

If you are uncomfortable writing your own newsletter, or do not have the time, you can hire a student to do it. I know people who have hired journalism students or reporters from college newspapers, who wanted the experience and extra money from undertaking such a project.

QUICK TIPS FOR SUCCESS

If your publicity is going to increase your sales and profits, you must sell the sizzle. Anything that sizzles is hot, and your business should also be hot. Publicity, by its nature, is highly complimentary, it sizzles with good news about your products/services. You want other people to know how wonderful your products/services are, so that they will become your customers or clients.

You should always make reprints of a positive story and send it, along with a solicitation letter and Rolodex card, to individuals who make up a targeted group of prospects. In all cases, you should get permission to reprint a story from the newspaper or magazine that published it.

You should purchase a mailing list of prospects from a professional list company, after you have given the company your criteria: age, profession, gender, location, etc.

If you are unsure about the contents and style of a letter, put together a focus group so that you can test the effectiveness of several different letters.

On a regular basis, you should do subsequent mailings that consist of brochures and newsletters. It is important that you regularly remind new and existing customers of who you are and what you do. To save money, you may want to get a bulk mail permit from your local post office.

Remember that all of these steps must be followed; to eliminate just one of the steps may mean that a prospect will escape your net.

Good luck.

And remember: Always sell the sizzle!

CHAPTER 4

Reach Out and Touch a Prospect: Closing Deals

You've planted your seeds. You've lovingly made sure that each seed was ideally placed and fertilized. You've watered each one. Now, it's time to harvest the results.

If all has gone according to plan, you have already had a response from some of your targeted publicity. Perhaps you have even received a few telephone calls from people who received your solicitation letters, Rolodex cards, and brochures.

In most cases, you can only expect a 1% to 3% response. To increase that response, you must turn the audience that received your direct mail package from passive recipients into active customers or clients.

They already know who you are and what you do. They have read about you in newspapers or magazines, they have read your solicitation letter, they have filed your Rolodex card, and they have read your brochure.

Now, it is time to reach out and touch each one of them. If you have the time, you can do it yourself. If not, you should hire college students and pay them an hourly rate to call each person who received your direct-mail package; since each person to be called is a potential customer, you want to meet with each one. Therefore, it is the job of your telephone solicitor to set up appointments, so that you can meet with people face to face, look each one in the eye, and close deals.

Whether you do the calling or you hire someone to do it for you, the telephone calls should not be improvised. There should be a standard telemarketing script for each call; the script should also have sufficient space to write notes.

Though I could write a sample telemarketing script for you, it is far more effective to write a script that reflects your style and personality so that you feel comfortable, sound personable and authentic, and can achieve your goals.

I will, however, provide a few guidelines: You must begin by asking to speak to a specific person. If you get a receptionist or secretary who asks who you are and wants to know the nature of your business, simply give your name, your company name, and say that it is a personal matter or that you have to talk to so-and-so personally.

MAKE AN OFFER THEY CAN'T REFUSE

Once you have introduced yourself, you must make an irresistible appeal, consisting of an offer that cannot be refused.

I have heard of countless small business owners saying something to the effect of the following: "Hi. This is Mr. Smith. I just opened a fabulous restaurant that serves the freshest fish and vegetables. Our desserts are all scrumptious, and we have a superb chef who was trained in France. Our tables have the most expensive linens, beautiful flat ware, aromatic center pieces. The ambience is sophisticated yet intimate. We have a romantic pianist who sings all the

71

old standards. Our wine cellar is second to none." This litany goes on and on, until the prospect finally hangs up.

Friends and relatives might feel proud at the description of such an obviously wonderful restaurant, and the owner certainly feels proud. Pride of ownership, however, is not an incentive for drawing in customers.

Rather than describing all of the wonderful attributes of your restaurant, if you were to invite potential diners to enjoy a free bottle of wine with their meal, or buy one entree and so get another for free, or benefit from some other giveaway, you would create an incentive that attracts customers as surely as a magnet attracts metal filings.

Whenever you call prospects, you must offer some kind of incentive that will interest them. Think of it as a form of fishing. You would not fish without bait, and you cannot get customers without bait. You must make sure that you can make good on your promises; never offer someone an incentive if you cannot deliver. Most businesses survive or perish on their reputations. Never do anything that will tarnish the reputation of your business.

Following are some examples.

"Call Your Mother For Free" Promotion

In 1988, I introduced a Swiss telephone into the United States. The telephone (called "Swisstel") was corded, weighed 3.5 ounces, and was half an inch thick. It came in an assortment of decorator colors. Altogether, it was quite attractive, but none of that would have caused a rush of sales. In order to introduce prospective customers to the phone, I decided to offer them something for nothing, something that would require using the phone. Once they used it, many of them would want to buy it.

Here's what I was able to arrange: Bloomingdale's department store, in New York City, agreed to introduce the telephone during one Mother's Day weekend. The store also agreed to give anyone who tried the phone a free, one-minute phone call to any place in the continental United States. Each person was invited to call his or her mother and wish her a happy Mother's Day.

Bloomingdale's advertised the promotion in order to attract prospective customers, and I sent out press releases to alert the media to the event. More than 10,000 people participated in the event, and thousands upon thousands of pleased participants purchased phones at $79.95 each. We had offered customers an attractive incentive, and they repaid our kindness with purchases. It was a powerfully effective incentive! Indeed, the client was so pleased he increased his monthly PR fee by almost 40%.

CAPITALIZE ON THE FEAR OF BEING FINED

I had a client who operated an OSHA compliance service. It ensured that factories were in compliance with all federal OSHA rules and regulations. Prior to calling potential customers, we assembled a list of companies that had failed their OSHA inspections and been fined. When each company was called, we carefully explained that we could help them avoid fines in the future and, in many cases, reduce existing fines. That was an intriguing incentive, and many of those called agreed to meet with my client. At the meetings, many of those companies retained my client's services.

LEVERAGE PEOPLE'S FEAR OF TAXES AND PENALTIES

I recognized a similar opportunity in the case of an accountant client, whose story I told in Chapter 1. He had assembled an extensive list of people who had tax liens against their property. Each person received a solicitation letter and an article that I had written for the accountant. When called, each recipient was told that their tax liens could be removed, often for a fraction of the actual liability. Each one was invited to come into the accountant's office for a free consultation. If, at that time, they were convinced the accountant could help them, they would pay a modest retainer. The accountant's practice, as you might expect, grew like a well-cared-for garden.

SHOW HOW LOSSES CAN PAY DIVIDENDS

Each business has the ability to offer an incentive, and many of those incentives are nothing more than what marketers call "loss leaders." A loss leader is an item that is sold at cost, given away, or sold at a steep discount, so that customers will come into a store and purchase other merchandise at full price. If your solicitation calls are going to be successful, you must offer prospects an incentive, a loss leader, something that they perceive as having real value.

SUCCESSFUL TELEPHONE SELLING

Once you have aroused the curiosity of prospects and appealed to their self-interest, you can tell them something about your business and answer whatever questions they may have. In fact, it is always a good idea to ask as many pertinent questions of a potential client as you can think of, for it shows a real interest on your part. Make sure that the questions are important, not just a polite attempt to draw a prospect into your orbit. Each question you ask should tell you something you didn't already know about a prospect's business. One question should naturally lead into the next. When you have finished asking your questions, you can make a summary generalization that shows off your understanding. The entire process will serve to cement a relationship between you and a prospect.

Whether you are a service business or a manufacturer, it is essential that you do not get off the telephone until you have made a specific appointment to visit the prospect. It is often at that appointment that you will have an opportunity to close a deal.

When selling to a prospect on the telephone, you must be careful to be neither too aggressive and pushy nor too tentative and relaxed. In the first instance, you will drive a prospect away; in the second instance, you will simply let a prospect lose interest and slip through your fingers. Mentally map a line between the two poles and try to sail your business into a port of success.

Personal warmth and charm will go a long way in opening doors and winning over prospects. Those qualities, however, must be genuine; there is nothing as disabling to a business relationship as an obvious lack of authenticity.

HIRING TELEPHONE MARKETERS

It is obviously essential that if you hire others to do telephone solicitations, they must be as interested in generating new business as you are. Before you hire, you should give each applicant a script, and audition them as carefully as if they were trying out for a Broadway play. Once you have made your choices, carefully rehearse your solicitors, then rehearse them again and again, and even again. Every aspect of the solicitation must be letter perfect; nothing should be left to chance.

I have said that your telephone solicitor should be as interested in generating new business as you are; however, few employees, unless they are very close relatives, will feel impelled to see you soar to new levels of success. In order to create a symbiotic relationship between your interests and those of the solicitor, you must create an attractive incentive. When I have set up telephone solicitations for my clients, I have always offered the solicitor a bonus for each appointment arranged; thereafter, the solicitor will receive a commission for each piece of new business, for each deal closed. No one, after all, enjoys working for a simple hourly wage; monetary incentives, however, will motivate many people to perform at their best. The most successful salespeople are those who increase their annual incomes through commissions. College students, especially, like having extra funds on hand for movies, dining, entertainment. It is difficult to accumulate a surplus of spending money by working for $6 an hour. If they can add a few hundred dollars to that every week or so, they will work very hard, indeed, to earn it.

You and the telephone solicitor should understand what the basic elements of a telephone solicitation are:

Step 1. Introduce yourself. This often includes getting past the barrier of a secretary or receptionist. It may also require eliciting the immediate interest of someone who otherwise has little or no interest in listening to you. Gently proceed. Do not politely accept rejection. Gracefully move forward.

Step 2. Offer an incentive. This often involves solving a problem that you know exists, offering a service below market cost, or providing something for free if something else is purchased.

Step 3. Ask intelligent questions. Draw out the prospect. Everyone likes to talk about their business, their success, their goals, etc. Ask if they are having any problems. Is there any help you can provide?

Step 4. Describe your business. You may provide a brief general description; however, specific details should directly relate to the prospect's business, so that obvious connections can be made.

Step 5. Ask if the prospect has any questions. Make sure your answers, like your descriptions, relate to the business interests of the prospect.

Step 6. Set up an appointment. If you have samples of products or a portfolio of work, let the prospect know that you will bring these with you, and ask if they would like you to bring anything else. If you are visiting a retailer, you may want to bring racks or display cases in addition to sample products. You might also bring along point-of-purchase promotional materials, table tents, counter displays, posters, etc.

Step 7. Confirm place, date, and time.

Step 8. If the prospect is unavailable for weeks or even months, ask when a good time to call back would be, enter the information on a calendar, and call back. In the interim, however, write letters, one saying how much you enjoyed speaking with them, another describing new services or products you have, and perhaps a third letter that lets them know of an important recent accomplishment.

Exhibit 4-1 is a sample letter that can be used as a first step in developing a positive relationship with someone who cannot immediately meet with you.

EXHIBIT 4-1   After a telephone solicitation, it is a good idea to set up a meeting time with the prospect. If meeting right away is impossible, write a letter (much like this one) explaining how you can be of service to this prospect.

Dear _____:

I very much enjoyed speaking with you and learning about your business. I particularly enjoyed hearing about XYZ. Here is some information that I have put together that relates to your own products (or services).

In addition, I have taken the liberty of enclosing a brochure about my company. I believe it briefly but fully explains our services/products. If, after reading it, you have any questions, please don't hesitate to call me. I shall be happy to answer whatever questions you may have. I have also enclosed my business card and a Rolodex card for your use.

I have noted on my calender to call you on (date). I look forward to speaking with you again, then getting together for a productive meeting during which I can show you how I can be of service to your business.

Cordially,

MEETING WITH PROSPECTIVE CUSTOMERS

Once you have arranged to meet with a prospect, you must have a well-rehearsed script in your head that will be essential in helping you to close deals.

Again, it is extremely important that you ask the kinds of questions that will tell you exactly what a prospect needs or wants. If, for example, they have no interest in flowers, but you can show them how to use flowers as a marketing device to increase sales, you have appealed to their self-interest.

I once had a client who owned a liquor store; his business had fallen off because so many people had stopped drinking hard liquor. Instead, people were drinking wine with dinner, water and juices at other times. The mixed drink or cocktail had passed into memory for many newly health-conscious people. He called me upon the recommendation of a former client, and told me that if he couldn't increase his business, he would have to give up half of his retail space.

Prior to meeting with me, he had met with other marketing public relations professionals. They had listened to his tale of woe, but they had not really heard him. Rather than understanding the diminishing market for hard liquor, they suggested ways of making liquor attractive through coupons, special sales, contests, promotions, even seminars on how to make successful mixed drinks. All of those ideas might have been effective if the size of the market had not been steadily shrinking; none of their ideas would convince someone to switch from grapefruit juice to bourbon!

The store owner was extremely disappointed, for no one had proposed charting a new marketing course, one that would take him into previously unexplored territory. Having listened closely to his problems, I decided not to attempt to generate additional sales of hard liquor, but to pursue other businesses that could use wine as a promotional tool for generating customer loyalty and additional sales.

I began by going to a stockbroker who had about 3,000 customers. I suggested that he send his best customers bottles of wine for their anniversaries, birthdays, children's graduations, etc. I could not only get him good bottles of wine at a discount, but I could also arrange for the liquor store to deliver them.

The stockbroker agreed, and my client now had more than 1,000 additional customers, who would also know the name of the store that had delivered the wine.

I was able to help that store owner because I went to my initial meeting without preconceived notions of marketing retail liquor products. I listened, I learned, and I was able to do something that increased my client's sales and profits. Indeed, like most good promotions, it benefited everyone involved: the wine merchant, the stockbroker, and me.

IF IT WORKS ONCE, IT WILL WORK AGAIN

I next went to an upscale car dealer who sold several models of luxury cars. I basically made the same suggestion to him that I had made to the stockbroker: send your customers bottles of wine on their birthdays and anniversaries. He had fewer customers than the stockbroker; nonetheless, we all benefited.

Altogether, the wine merchant was able to compensate for the loss of hard liquor sales by selling and delivering wine to people who had never been in or even near his store.

THE KEY IS LISTENING

The worst salespeople are those who do not take the time to listen to potential customers: they simply launch their sales pitches, never wondering for a moment if their prospects want or need what they are selling.

A good salesperson, by contrast, listens closely to the needs of potential customers, then fashions a product or service that satisfies those needs.

COLD CALLS OR CALLS TO HELP

I regularly get cold calls from stockbrokers asking me to buy stocks, bonds, mutual funds, etc. Not one of them has ever taken the time to ask me what I want, and I have never given one of them any of my business.

A different sort of stockbroker came to me; he wanted to build a customer base, but did not want to spend many hours every day making cold calls to lists of nearly anonymous people.

We decided that since Congress had eliminated the standard deductions for IRAs, we would show people how much they could still save by opening various kinds of IRAs. I wrote an advertisement that appeared in an investment publication. It read: "EARN MILLIONS FOR YOUR RETIREMENT. FREE SEMINAR. NO OBLIGATION. Call for appointment. Seating limited."

Nearly 300 people attended the seminar that we held in a school. My client demonstrated how various sums of money (ranging from $1,000 to $10,000) would grow each year, for twenty and thirty years, in a variety of investments. He also revealed how much money people at various income levels (ranging from $50,000 to $100,000) were spending on vacations, dinners, and entertainment. If they invested a fraction of that money and rolled it over every year, they could have substantial savings when they retired. And they would not experience any significant drop in their style of living by investing from $1,000 to $5,000 every year. About 10% of those in attendance became his customers; we did similar seminars on a regular basis, until word of mouth alone began to make him successful.

My point is that my client succeeded because he had an audience of people who were interested in saving for their retirement. He had listened to the concerns of others, and so he was able to propose precise solutions. He addressed their needs and showed them how affordable a cushy retirement could be. The need and the solution came together, and both were successful.

NEVER LET THEM FORGET YOU

When meeting with a prospect, you should also have several "leave-behinds" that will be a regular and impressive reminder of your business.

Examples of "leave-behinds" that I generally prepare for clients follow.

1. A four-color brochure or sell sheet. If you have a service business, the brochure should highlight the kinds of services that you provide. You should emphasize the nature of those services so that they do not mimic those of your competitors; rather, your services should be special and unique. If it is a product brochure, it should list all of your products in their manifold varieties. You may also list prices and delivery services, as well as other qualities that distinguish you from your competition. Whatever you do, do not produce a black-and-white brochure. It will invariably look cheap and not show you off to your best advantage.

The photos in your brochure should show off those things that will most impress people about your business. In some instances, it will contain photos of your products imaginatively arranged. If you have a service business, the brochure should have photos of you carrying out various tasks for clients. In fact, the photos can tell the story of your services, illustrating each step of the various projects that you carry out for clients.

The brochure should, of course, have your name, address, and telephone number. Exhibit 4-2a and b shows sample sell sheets; Exhibits 4-3 and 4-4 are reprints of ads; and Exhibit 4-5 is a product sheet; all of these were used as leave-behinds.

2. Rolodex card and business card. Even though you have previously sent a Rolodex and business card, leave an additional one of each. The Rolodex card, as I noted in Chapter 3, should have a tab that symbolically distinguishes the nature of your business, so that it is immediately recognizable in the prospect's Rolodex.

EXHIBIT 4-2a   Sell sheets are a good way to advertise the types of services or products that you provide. This is a sample sell sheet for Professional Foot Care Products.

PROFESSIONAL Sets Record Sales & Profits.
FOOT CARE PRODUCTS

A major national mass merchandiser challenged us to prove our claims that our unique foot care program generates sales and profits far above average. After 182 days on site, the results are in.

PROFESSIONAL FOOT CARE SELLS!
During the test period, over 2200 units were sold. The average unit sale was $3.85, clearly well above average for foot care products.

PROFESSIONAL FOOT CARE BRINGS IN THE PROFITS!
Total sales for the test period were over $8,500.00 which grossed over $3,400.00 in profits. These profits did not take away from other foot care product sales.

PROFESSIONAL FOOT CARE INVENTORY TURNS FAST!
Inventory turns are a key factor in determining profitability. Our merchandise showed an average of greater than 4 turns in 182 days. This projects to over 9 turns per year. These impressive results were achieved using our proven merchandising techniques.

COMBINED ACTUAL 182-DAY SALES RESULTS CHART*

PROFESSIONAL PRODUCT	PIECES SOLD	RETAIL VALUE	40% PROFIT
Product A	578 units	$1,439.22	$575.69
Product B	299 units	$ 834.21	$333.68
Product C	272 units	$1,085.28	$434.11
Product D	173 units	$ 863.27	$345.31
Product E	164 units	$ 654.36	$261.74
Product F	159 units	$ 634.41	$253.76
Product G	148 units	$ 590.52	$236.21
Product H	135 units	$ 673.65	$269.46
Product I	122 units	$ 852.78	$341.11
Product J	85 units	$ 339.15	$135.66
Product K	82 units	$ 573.18	$229.27
	2217 units	$8,540.03	$3,416.00

*Average Sale: $3.85; Average Turn: 4.2 (182 days).

PROFESSIONAL
FOOT CARE PRODUCTS
A division of PROfessional PROduct Research Co. Inc.
74 20th Street, Brooklyn, NY 11232
PHONE: (718) 768-7383 • FAX: (718) 768-7151

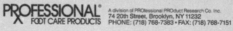

EXHIBIT 4-2b   Another sample sell sheet.

P.O.P. EDUCATES CONSUMER

Foot care, for the most part, is an impulse sale. And, there's nothing like a strong, full color visual to grab attention and stimulate your customer's response. That's why we ship an illustrated Point of Purchase (P.O.P.) header card with every Professional Foot Care product program. It indicates a common foot problem, the correct professional product to relieve it

and the key words to indicate the solution. The consumer then, has all the information needed to quickly and easily make the right selection.

The same problem/product/solution graphics are also carried forward to the packaging to reinforce the P.O.P. selling message.

HIGH QUALITY UNIQUE PRODUCTS

The Professional Foot Care Product Line consists of the highest quality products not found in traditional foot care displays. Our products do not overlap or conflict with your existing programs — so now you can expand this important category without detracting any sales from your established merchandise offerings.

Each product addresses a specific foot ailment that is common to over 80% of your customers. Our Donut Heel Pad™ is one example. This unique, soft foam pad supports sensitive heel areas and has a removable center circle that gently surrounds and cushions painful heel spurs. Other products like our Heel Cushion, Gentle Step™ 3/4 Insoles, Arch Lifter™ and ProClearz™ Antifungal Liquid, aid in reducing

pain and discomfort caused by overuse, abuse or malformation of the foot.

For more than 15 years, Professional has built its fine reputation by emphasizing quality, dependability, value and service.

PROFITABLE MERCHANDISING

Our strong merchandising programs pay off because they have mass appeal. Here's why you'll see results, realize new business, and earn maximum profits with Professional Foot Care Products.

- Higher Profit margins
- Increased dollar amount per sale
- Proven top movers
- In-store service merchandising
- Non-duplicate products

- Fewer SKU's
- Educational P.O.P. Headers
- Co-op advertising
- Consumer support programs
- Products satisfy consumer needs

PUT PROFESSIONAL TO WORK FOR YOU

Professional Foot Care offers you 2 major benefits with its merchandised program — increased sales and increased profits in an increasing market. If you're tired of accepting sales based on a few

popular products and want every inch of your foot care Plan-O-Gram working at top dollar for you, it's time to put Professional Foot Care Products to work for you. Call or Write today!

PROFESSIONAL®
X FOOT CARE PRODUCTS
A division of PROfessional PROduct Research Co. Inc.
74 20th Street, Brooklyn, NY 11232
(718) 768-7383   FAX: (718) 768-7151

---

3. Reprints of all of your print publicity. Assemble these into a folder. There should also be a page listing all of the radio and television publicity that you have gotten. Finally, there should be testimonials from satisfied customers, each acclaiming you to the stars.

EXHIBIT 4-3 Reprints of advertisements can also be used by sales reps to help promote a product.

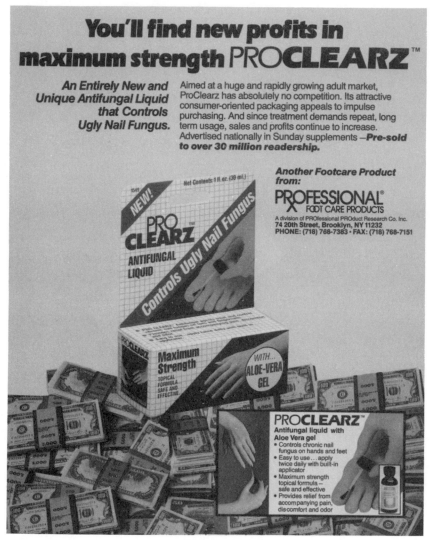

4. Free samples. If you sell products, bring along a free, inexpensive sample of something that is connected to your business. Cosmetic regularly mail prospective customers samples of soap, toothpaste, lotions, colognes, etc. You may also present a VIP coupon that gives a steep discount on one of your products.

EXHIBIT 4-4   Another reprint of another ad, used as a sales tool.

5. Your company newsletter. In Chapter 3, I noted how important a newsletter is to keeping your name before prospects. Bring along the most recent copy of your newsletter, and ask if the prospects would like to be put on your mailing list for future issues.

EXHIBIT 4-5 Product sheets are very helpful to buyers, and sales reps can leave them behind with prospective buyers as order forms.

PROFESSIONAL®
FOOT CARE PRODUCTS
74 20th Street, Brooklyn, NY 11232 • 718-768-7383 • Fax 718-768-7151

PRODUCT SHEET

SCISSORS

TOENAIL SCISSORS. #2111
A 4" long shank provides the extra leverage needed to cut toughest toenails easily. Made of hot dropped forged carbon steel, stays sharp. For regular and thick toenails.

TOENAIL NIPPER. #1001
Clips ingrown nails safely. Curved blade slips under ingrown nails, avoids painful pulling. Made from surgical steel. Stays sharp.

SUPER SCISSOR. #3758
The curved one inch blade safely clips even the toughest toenails easily. A six inch long shank does the reaching so you have no bending or straining. Serrated edges stay sharp, made of surgical steel.

HEEL PRODUCTS

HEEL CUSHIONS. #5328
Soft molded rubber heel cushions featuring rubber nodules that help relieve foot pain, leg fatigue, heel spurs and shin splints. One size fits all. One pair.

HEEL GRIPS. #1075
Soft rubber adhesive back Heel Snugs make loose heels fit better. Prevents slipping and rubbing of the heel. One pair fits all size shoes.

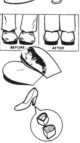

WALK-RIGHT.™ #5894-5896
A wedge shaped layer pad made of molded rubber and leather that restores body balance by distributing weight equally. Removes pressure from ankles, feet and legs. Helps prevent uneven wear on the heels of shoes. Worn invisibly in shoes. All sizes fit both men & women. One pair.

HIGH HEEL SAVERS. #4891
Plastic caps slip over high heels for safer walking. Protects heel from wearing down. Keeps shoes looking like new—longer. Two pair in two sizes fits 90% of high heels.

HEEL PRODUCTS

DONUT HEEL PADS. #1107-1108
Relieves painful heel spurs. Specially designed soft foam pads cushions sensitive heel area to ease painful pressure. Removable center circle surrounds and cushions heel spur. Men and women sizes.

INSOLES

FOAM CUSHION INSOLES. #5071
Unique two-layer design features brush nylon top for comfort and a foam bottom base for shock absorption. Excellent for use in all shoes.

THERMAL FLEECE INSOLES. #6020
Specially designed two-layer construction provides double insulation for extra warmth and comfort. Acrylic fleece top keeps feet warm and dry in cold, damp weather, while foam bottom gently cushions every step. One size fits all; trim chart included. One pair.

GENTLE-STEP™ 3/4 INSOLES. #1090-1095
Gives gentle support to feet. Reduce foot fatigue and walk in comfort. Perforations through smooth comfort top allow feet to breathe and stay dry. Special foam inserts give added support to arch and cushions metatarsal. One pair. Sizes for both men and women.

PROmold™ SHOE AND SNEAKER INSERTS. #5334-5337
Specially designed 3 layer insole cushions and supports feet. Controls shock and molded heel provides heel stability. Soft memory foam terry top absorbs perspiration and middle layer is activated with charcoal to control foot odors. Fits all shoes and sneakers. One pair. Sized to fit both men and women.

Obviously, a prospect will be impressed with all these items. Such preparedness shows not only that you care about generating new business, but that you take considerable pride in your business and accomplishments. In other words, you want to make a sale, but you also want to express your pride. If you weren't the proprietor of an excellent business, you would not want to show it off.

After your meeting, send the prospect a letter similar to the one in Exhibit 4-6.

EXHIBIT 4-6 It is a good idea to write a letter to your prospect after the two of you have met. Here is an example of the type of letter you might write.

Dear Mr. X:

I certainly enjoyed meeting with you, and appreciate your giving me so much of your valuable time. I'm sure that I can help the Custom Car Salon increase sales and develop greater depths of customer loyalty. Indeed, I believe that each of your customers would enjoy receiving a bottle of Voodoo Magic Red Wine on their birthdays and anniversaries.

I have arranged for a bottle to be sent to you and know that you will enjoy it.

If you would like to test my proposed promotion on a select number of customers for a period of, let's say, three months, I believe you will be pleased by the positive results.

I look forward to working with you, and I will call you next week to learn when you want to get started. If, at any time, you have any questions, please don't hesitate to contact me.

Kind regards,

QUICK TIPS FOR SUCCESS

Remember that all the steps I have gone through in this chapter must be followed; to eliminate just one of the steps may mean that a prospect will escape your net.

If you are going to be an effective telephone marketer, you must always listen to the needs and concerns of your prospective customers. Listen to their problems, then figure out how your products/services can provide solutions, meet their needs, and give them what they are looking for.

Whether selling retirement annuities or cases of wine, you must gear your sales and marketing techniques to the interests of your customers.

If you do not have the time to make telephone solicitation calls yourself, hire a college student to make them.

Whether you or a student makes the calls, you should always use a script; yet you should always leave room for spontaneous interaction. The calls should be made about ten days after you have mailed your direct mail packages. The point of each call is to set up an appointment.

At your meetings, try to close deals. Have additional copies of your publicity reprints and brochures to leave with prospects. You should also leave behind brochures, newsletters, Rolodex cards, business cards, and (if you are selling products) sell sheets.

After each meeting, write a letter thanking the prospect for becoming a customer, or saying that you will contact them again in the future. Keep a file of notes about each of your meetings. Some people will need to be called in the future, some will be written off, and others will have made the entire endeavor worthwhile by becoming customers.

CHAPTER 5

Promoting New Business To Get Newer Business

Now that you have gotten new business, it is essential to use that accomplishment to generate even newer business. Remember, you must spend 50% of your time generating new business, and 50% of your time servicing the business you have. Any business that does not continue to generate new business eventually goes out of business; and, as soon as you get new business, you are on your way to losing that business. It is simply the nature of the business world (if not the whole world) that nothing lasts forever, and everything must eventually be replenished.

Everyone likes to be part of a success story, so you must make yourself appear as successful as possible. After all, if you are successful, you must be doing a host of things right, and you must have knowledge and skills that many other people would also like to have. Success is like honey, failure like vinegar: one draws by its very sweetness, the other repels.

GETTING NEW BUSINESS: AN EXAMPLE

How does one turn new business into a solicitation for still newer business? Let me give you an example.

In the Introduction and Chapter 1, I wrote briefly about two women who opened their own commercial interior design company. One of the first commissions I helped them to get was a building that was being converted into shoe showrooms and offices. While they were working to complete that commission, they had no time to solicit new business. However, I had been hired to do just that.

Once they began working on their new commission, I sent out a press release to all of the real estate and shoe publications, announcing that my client had been hired to complete a million-dollar-plus interior design commission. It was, indeed, an enviable plum, especially for a new company. I prepared a brochure for my client, and wrote the first in a series of quarterly newsletters. I made reprints of the press release as it had appeared in a real estate publication, and mailed it to building managers and shoe companies; I also included a copy of the brochure. Two weeks later, I mailed out a complimentary issue of the newsletter to each of the earlier recipients. More than 1,500 prospects were now aware of my client's activities, their success, and the promising future of their company.

A number of building managers began recommending my client's services to new tenants, especially ones for whom they would have to build showrooms.

As my client continued to work on many shoe showrooms and offices, I publicized special rooms that they created. For example, they created a magnificent entertainment center at the top of the first shoe-showroom building. It included state-of-the-art video and audio equipment, with a multiplicity of viewing options (ranging from screens of varying sizes, to color-coded lighting to alter the room's ambience) and special sound effects (such as wind, rain, and waterfalls). This was all heightened by an indoor water fountain and a waterfall on the nearby roof garden. I wrote a press release about the sophisticated, nearly magical, entertainment room. It appeared in several real estate publications.

I hired a well-known interior design photographer to document the magnificent interior. I eventually showed his photos to an interior design magazine, which decided to do a feature story about the building.

When the job was near completion, I wrote a celebratory advertisement. I showed it to my client's client, the shoe company, and they approved (since it benefited them as well). In the text, the shoe company thanked my client for doing a superb job. My client paid for the ad, which ran in various trade publications.

I next wrote a case history about how the job was handled and completed. This was mailed, along with the ad and a solicitation letter, to about 750 shoe companies in New York, New Jersey, Pennsylvania, and Connecticut. The standard follow-up phone calls were made by a college student working from a telemarketing script that I had written. This resulted in three additional shoe showroom clients at very handsome fees! I had not only sold the sizzle, but I had created several new sizzles that could also be sold. The process is one that goes on and on, for as long as a business lasts.

The lesson to be learned from this project is that if your accomplishments are celebrated and promoted to other prospects, then you will have an excellent chance of getting new business.

We see this process all the time in the medical profession: if a doctor saves the lives of patients suffering from a particular illness, and the doctor's work is reported in the media, then other patients will flock to the doctor's care.

INCREASING THE POPULARITY OF RETAIL PRODUCTS

A process similar to the one that I've just described (for a service business) can be applied to a manufacturer. As I've previously related, Professional Foot Care Products decided in 1990 to expand from exclusively mail-order into retail business. I provided marketing assistance to the company's national sales manager by generating new product stories in retail trade publications; as a result of my efforts, he was able to get products into a few retail chains.

There were, however, many other chains that could have taken the products, but had not done so. One way to convince those other chains to carry our products was to let them know that their competitors were doing so, and were enjoying brisk sales. Therefore, each time that a well-known retail chain took our products, I sent out a press release trumpeting the news, which often resulted in the publication of an article in one of the trade magazines. Exhibits 5-1, 5-2, and 5-3 show three such articles. I also quoted the sales manager, predicting how much business the chain would do by selling our products. Reprints of those stories were sent to buyers at the other chains, and the national sales manager called upon those buyers with copies of the stories, sell sheets, samples, and order forms. In addition, we sent out one-page letters every month, letting buyers know who was selling our products and how well they were doing. The obvious message was that they had to get on the bandwagon if they, too, wanted to enjoy rapid turns and high profits.

If Kmart, for example, took the products and was enjoying brisk sales and increased revenue, then so should Walmart, Caldor, and

EXHIBIT 5-1 Reprints of articles can help gain new business: this article promotes the fact that Kmart is now carrying the product.

Proclearz Fungicide Carried by Kmart

NEW YORK—Proclearz, a topical treatment that controls nail fungus, is now being sold in Kmart Corp. stores.

"We have worked long and hard to get Proclearz in the Kmart chain, and we believe that this new association will be good for both Kmart and our company," says John Vayianos, vice president and national sales manager for Professional Foot Care Products,

which manufactures the antifungal liquid.

"As a mail-order product Proclearz had been selling 500,000 units a year. Once we introduced the product into drug chains and mass market merchandisers the product really took off and sold better than any of our other products."

Proclearz' niche category has expanded to include many people who wear running shoes and sneakers, as well as women who use artificial nails.

"We've put a lot of money into advertising Proclearz, and it is obviously paying off," says Leonard Feldman, president of the company.

The firm manufactures more than 30 items, all of which are sold in drug stores, sporting goods stores and mass market outlets.

EXHIBIT 5-2 Another reprint of another article used to gain new business.

Walgreen Outlets Feature Proclearz Treatment Line

NEW YORK—Professional Foot Care Products' best-selling item, Proclearz, an over-the-counter antifungal treatment for fingernails and toenails, has made its debut in all 1,564 Walgreen Co. stores.

The line's niche has expanded

"The product quickly became a best-seller shortly after we introduced it, and it sells far better than any other competitive product," says Professional Foot Care Products president and chief executive officer Leonard Feldman.

In the past the product's market had been people aged 45 and over, who suffer from nail fungus more often than younger people, according to vice president and national sales manager John Vayianos. "Now, however," he says, "its niche category has expanded to include all people who wear running shoes and sneakers, because their feet perspire profusely, and their shoes provide little if any ventilation.

"In addition, all those women who adhere artificial nails to their fingernails are prime candidates for nail fungus."

An untreated nail fungus may ultimately lead to a costly and sometimes unsuccessful nail extraction.

More than 20 million people annually suffer from varying degrees of nail fungus, according to Vayianos. Proclearz' price, at about $7, compares favorably with similar products selling for up to $14.

Sears. Each mass-market retailer and chain drugstore will carry products that another store is selling, if the products are successfully generating profits. All it takes is convincing them that they should get on the bandwagon; in order to do that, one has to hype one's success. It often requires sending out press releases, direct-mail pieces, newsletters, and personalized letters, and making phone calls, etc.

Whenever we did it, we got the results we wanted. In fact, after three years, there wasn't a drugstore chain, superstore, or mass-market retail chain that didn't carry my client's products. They all wanted to be part of the success that their competitors were

EXHIBIT 5-3 Successful marketing helps a business mushroom: this is another reprint of an article based on a press release.

Proclearz Push

NEW YORK—Professional Foot Care Products has announced that Snyder Drug Stores Inc. will sell the vendor's antifungal nail product.

Snyder's has more than 100 outlets in Wisconsin and Minnesota. Proclearz, which retails for from $4.99 to $6.99, is a topical treatment.

Professional Foot Care Products will continue its push into retail outlets and step up its print campaign in major national magazines. The company says that 20 million people annually suffer from varying degrees of nail fungus.

enjoying. And we had made that success dramatic and exciting through our marketing-oriented public relations.

If you have a product that you are trying to sell to retailers, you can do the same thing. Make others feel as if they should be part of your success. Invite them to the party.

PROFESSIONAL PRACTICES MARKET TRACK RECORDS OF SUCCESS

And what if you are a lawyer or head hunter—or even a marketing guru?

One of my clients is a famous lawyer who represents many of the best-known names in corporate America. He has negotiated successful conclusions to some of the most difficult union strikes in the last decade and a half. His clients do not like him to talk publicly about his work, for they do not want the world to know that they have labor problems. My client, however, is free to talk about company XYZ as a fictional example of a company with labor problems; or about specific labor issues (such as sexual harassment in the workplace, job discrimination, age discrimination, termination for cause, and many other issues).

On one occasion, he had settled a labor dispute for a major American manufacturing company. Though he could not mention his client specifically, he could talk about labor issues in general, particularly those that were troubling his client and had caused their unionized workers to go on strike. I got my client on a national television news program where he addressed the issues faced by his client. He never mentioned his client by name, and when the moderator did, my client never acknowledged that his own client had been the point of reference. He simply spoke authoritatively about the labor issues involved, and about how various problems could be solved. As a result of his appearance, he signed up a major corporation as a new client. It was another way of selling the sizzle, and it was done without directly taking credit for that sizzle.

PROMOTE THYSELF

Even I have sold myself as if I were my own client, which in a sense I am.

On one occasion, I wrote an article for a business publication. The article was entitled "How To Market and Promote Your Small Business." I also took out a 1/8-page display ad on the page opposite my article. In the article, I wrote about what I had done for several of my clients, refraining from mentioning them by name for fear that someone else might go after their business. I enumerated everything I had done for them, and how I had turned their aborning or stagnating businesses into substantial successes. In the ad, I noted that I could increase the sales and profits of many small businesses, and offered a free consultation. The border of the ad was set off with dollar signs. Though I received many calls, I also decided to buy a list of recently incorporated businesses in New York

City. I mailed each one a copy of my article and the ad; I enclosed a covering letter, a business card, and a Rolodex card. The response was so enormous that I had to hire another person to help me with all the new business!

I further publicized my efforts by figuring out how small businesses can seem larger than they really are. I put together a list of points and sent the list to *Home Office Computing* magazine which ran a major story. Again, the response was so positive that a television program called *The Wall Street Journal Reports* did an extensive interview with me on the subject, and the program aired throughout the United States.

People are invariably impressed by one's ability to create hoopla, to make a sow's ear into a silk purse. Watching Bill Clinton's 1992 inauguration, I noticed that he hugged everyone who approached him. I called a reporter at the *Daily News*, Lenore Skenazy, and told her that I was the one who had given President Clinton the idea to hug people at his inauguration.

"How did you do that?" she asked.

"My office is down the street from the Intercontinental Hotel where Clinton stayed while in New York," I responded. "I was walking by one day, and there was Bill on the street shaking the hands of well-wishers. I went over to him and, instead of shaking his hand, I gave him a hug. He was so impressed that he decided to hug everyone else from that moment forward. It was all my idea!"

Lenore Skenazy subsequently wrote a story for the Daily News, entitled "Hugga Bubba," in which she quoted me as giving Bill Clinton the idea to hug well-wishers at his inauguration. Of course, she mentioned that I was a New York City marketing professional.

Here is what she wrote: "'Actually, Clinton got the idea of hugging from me,' claims Jeffrey Sussman, president of the Manhattan marketing firm that bears his name. 'When he was here for the New York primary, I saw him on the street by the Intercontinental Hotel and there were lots of people shaking his hand, but he seemed like a huggable guy, so I gave him a hug.'"

"And...? 'Well, he's a little on the heavy side, so you can't get your hands all the way around him, but he seemed very relaxed.' Would you hug him again? 'Why not?'"

A number of people called me after the story appeared and asked, "Is it really true?" "Are you kidding?"

Next, I decided to expand on that original story. I wrote a press release headlined, "New York P.R. Man Taught Bill Clinton to Hug!" I sent it to a nationally syndicated newspaper and magazine writer named Jeff Zaslow, who writes for the *Chicago Sun Times* as well as for *USA Weekend*. His delightful newspaper columnn, "All that Zazz," is syndicated to newspapers throughout the United States.

He wrote an entire column about me and what I had done (see Exhibit 5-4). He even mentioned that I should receive a presidential medal in the White House. He suggested that if President Clinton began hugging people in the Rose Garden to cheer them up, it would—no doubt—have been Sussman's idea. Brilliant! The article led to stories in other newspapers, as well as some cute, tongue-in-cheek TV news stories.

The point, of course, was that if I could publicize myself with such a zany PR coup, then just imagine what I could do for others. The point got across loud and clear, and numerous people asked me if I could do for them what I had done for myself. I said that, of course, I would try. And for many people, I succeeded.

TESTIMONIALS AND ENDORSEMENTS

Self-congratulation is always an important method of selling one-self; however, the self-congratulations must always seem to originate with someone else. Self-congratulation is never convincing if it is self-generated; indeed, it is perceived as being in exceedingly bad taste. It would be like a candidate nominating himself for a run at office. Ambitious and successful politicians always arrange to have others put their names in nomination, then act surprised and grateful.

EXHIBIT 5-4 Your product is not the only thing worth promoting—think about promoting yourself too. Jeffrey Sussman promoted himself by being the first well-wisher to give President Clinton a hug. Sussman's action prompted Jeff Zaslow of the *Chicago Sun Times* to write an entire column about the man who "taught Bill Clinton to hug!"

All that Zazz

'Hug' Launches Search For Pop Culture's Heroes

It was a hot day many years ago. You were thirsty, so you bought a Pepsi, took a swig, and then you said it: "You've got the right one, baby." After you swallowed, you issued a burp that sounded like: "Uh-huh!"

This was years before Ray Charles cashed in with the same sentiment. Now you're kicking yourself, knowing that you coined a phrase that many Americans can't get out of their heads without surgery.

Think back. There may be other omnipresent slogans, trends or cultural fads that you thought of first and aren't getting proper credit for. Way back when, didn't you refer to some of your internal organs—liver, spleen, heart, etc.—as "achy breaky?"

And when you were in kindergarten, didn't it cross your mind that everything you needed to know, you were learning right there from Mrs. Whatever-her-name-was? If that opportunist, Robert Fulghum, hadn't swiped your idea, you could have made millions writing *All I Really Need to Know I Learned in Kindergarten.*

Just days ago, a fellow named Jeffrey Sussman was like you—too bashful to take credit for something that he brought to the world. But now Sussman has stepped forward to accept our applause. You can, too.

Sussman is a New York public relations man who sometimes calls me seeking publicity for his clients. But now, he is publicizing himself. He has issued a press release: "THE CLINTON HUG STARTED BY N.Y. PR MAN."

"Remember all the hugging by President Clinton at the inauguration?" the release asks. "Who planted the idea? Who started the chain reaction of all those televised hugs?"

Who? Sussman.

It turns out that last year, he was in a line of everyday New Yorkers waiting to meet candidate Clinton. Everyone else shook Clinton's hand politely. But Sussman gave him a warm hug.

"He hugged me back," Sussman recalls. "He gave me a little perfunctory hug."

But Sussman could tell Clinton was moved. "It must have impressed him,"

Jeffrey Zaslow

says Sussman, "because he started hugging all those other people in Washington."

Isn't it possible that Clinton's propensity for hugging began long before Sussman came into his life? "Of course it is," Sussman allows. "But I'm claiming I gave him the idea. Why? Because I'm a PR man."

Sussman says he's tired of living in the background, pushing other people's achievements. "I want to come into the foreground," he says.

And what does he want for giving Clinton the hug idea? "A presidential award would be nice," says Sussman. "A Medal of Freedom. Whatever."

Sussman contacted the Wall Street Journal with his press release. The newspaper interviewed him, but never ran the story. (Perhaps they tracked down Arkansans like Gennifer Flowers, who claimed *they* taught Clinton how to hug.)

Now Sussman has given me an exclusive.

"Clinton really does know how to feel people's pain," Sussman says. "He may even be able to hug away their pain. I think he should forget about making promises he may not be able to keep. Instead, he should devote every Wednesday to hugging whoever is feeling sad or depressed. They could come to Washington, stand around in the Rose Garden for a while, get a really good presidential hug, then go home feeling terrific.

"A weekly presidential hug could go a long way to alleviating the nation's problems, giving people a sense of being loved, valued, appreciated and all that other good psychological stuff."

Well, now it's on record. When Clinton starts giving weekly Rose Garden hugs, Sussman can prove it was his idea.

Now, back to the rest of you.

I'd like to give credit where credit is due. If you've made a giant, unrecognized contribution to pop culture, let me know. I'll take your word for it—and print your claim in the column.

As the man who first thought Brooke Shields and Michael Jackson would make a cute couple, I know what it's like to energize the world, etc. So let's hear from you. Write: "It Was Me!" c/o Zazz, Box 3455, Chicago 60654.

Years ago, I was hired to publicize the book of an unknown writer who had some brilliant ideas. Most people, however, would not take him at his word—they required the reassurance of recognized authorities. Therefore, I solicited the opinions of well-known business leaders. I sent each one a prepublication copy of the manuscript, and asked them to read it; and if they agreed with what the author had to say, to please provide a testimonial for the back cover of the book. Even famous business leaders like to see themselves quoted in print; all but a handful were happy to provide the kind of testimonials that not only would have made the author's mother happy, but also helped to make the book a bestseller.

While I was publicizing *The World Almanac & Book of Facts* in 1984, I received testimonials from a wide assortment of celebrities, including one from then–Vice President George Bush. All of them wanted to see their names associated with *The World Almanac*.

Whether you are an aspiring author or have a small business, testimonials are an effective selling device—one that can inspire a positive word-of-mouth public relations campaign that results in one new piece of business after another.

GIVING AND GETTING AWARDS

Another way of getting testimonials is to give a prominent citizen an award and then let that person pay you back in kind. For example, I represented a small construction company that had built more than 1,000 units of low-income housing. It did so without direct government subsidies. Instead, it built the houses on abandoned land that was given to it by New York City. The government was happy to have someone turn that property into tax-generating property—after all, the government loves anything that will generate taxes.

My client performed its work without any help from politicians; I realized, however, that they could get much more work if politicians thought there might be some glory in the project for themselves. I contacted the Congressman in whose district the houses were built, and told him that we wanted to give him an award for all the support he had provided us—of course, he was happy to take the credit. I called a news conference, had my client present the congressman with an award, and the congressman then complimented my client not only for helping to provide housing for people who could not have otherwise afforded such housing, but also for building such high-quality homes for such modest prices.

The message was not lost on representatives from other congressional districts, especially when they saw the quantity of television coverage my client had obtained.

HONORED BY THE GOVERNMENT

If you have done something worthwhile for your community, you should arrange to get an award for your activities. This may require a friend to act as an intermediary, so that you do not put yourself in the embarrassing position of soliciting an award for yourself.

In 1981, I was a press secretary to a New York City Councilman. Everyday, I witnessed people coming into his office, offering sums of money, large and small, if he would declare a particular day in honor of them or one of their associates. He never did, but various other council representatives did. For those who received such honors, there was an obvious marketing advantage.

Similarly, if one has a good relationship with one's congressional representative, that person will graciously place a favorable mention of you into the Congressional Record. The words will not have been spoken, but the words of commendation will—nevertheless—appear in the printed Congressional Record with the federal logo atop the page. Reprints of that, when distributed to prospective customers, can be as effective as any award that the congressional representative might have given you in person.

MAKE YOUR PRODUCT AN AWARD

If you have a product that can be presented to public figures, for some generous acts that they have performed, you will reach many thousands of consumers who may not have otherwise heard of your product. As I related in Chapter 1, I used this technique to get free publicity for a client who manufactured models of Yankee Stadium. Despite the fact that theirs was the only architecturally accurate model of Yankee Stadium—and that every Yankee fan would want to own one—radio and television programs would not have given them the time of day. I hit upon a way of getting them an enormous amount of free publicity, however, by honoring people who didn't necessarily deserve to be honored.

No celebrity is so self-satisfied that he or she will refuse to be honored, especially if the honoring takes place in front of their own audience. Every public honor that proves what great human beings they are will not be turned aside. Each of the radio and television hosts not only accepted my clients on their shows and accepted (gratefully) a model of Yankee Stadium, but each also praised the model as if it were a gift from the gods. They went further and repeated several times my client's 800 number and urged their viewers or listeners to purchase the stadium.

Here are some ideas to get you thinking about further possibilities: Soaps for those who clean away graffiti; paint brushes for those who maintain the beauty of neighborhoods; food for those who are hungry; blankets for the cold and the homeless; pets for the lonely; posters to hang on the walls of people in welfare hotels. Virtually anything can be turned into an award and thereby generate publicity and good will for your products.

AWARDS CAN GROOM YOU FOR SUCCESS

Giving and getting awards is a gimmick of old-fashioned press agents. But, it works! Many years ago, I represented a trade association of dry cleaners. Each year, we asked the members to choose the Best Groomed Americans. Such people, we were careful to emphasize, were not necessarily the best dressed, but they evidenced great care in their personal appearance. Each year, we named ten celebrities as recipients of the award, and received a bounty of publicity. At the head of our annual list was one person whose total number of votes far exceeded all the rest. One year, for example, Johnny Carson topped the list. It was noted on the front page of *USA Today*, and he mentioned it during one of his monologues on the *Tonight Show*. Another year, President Reagan was named, and the announcement received national news coverage. What's more, we presented the president with a plaque, and he subsequently declared the month of April to be Good Grooming Month. Neighborhood cleaners were basking in the good will that had been generated on their behalf.

You, too, can put together a contest and then name public figures for awards. As public figures, they can provide you with excellent publicity, and their cooperation does not have to be solicited. They are, after all, in the public domain—and anyone can give them an award by sending out a press release.

EVERYBODY LOVES PETS

If your business can have a natural tie-in with pets, you have the beginnings of an appealing awards program. Here's what I did a number of years ago to help promote a pet shop.

The store owner was very careful to buy his puppies from individual breeders who were not running breeding factories. He was a man apart from many others in his line of work, and I wanted to publicize his good intentions and high standards. I assembled a group of local dog owners, and we formed the National Association for Healthy Puppies. We decided that we would give awards to the pet retailers who provided only the healthiest possible pups for sale to the public. Our one and only year in existence, we gave an award to my client, who also happened to deserve the award. We had a lunch for him, to which everyone brought their dogs. There were dog biscuits for the pets, sandwiches for their owners. The honoree received a large brass dog biscuit with his name engraved on one side—it even had its own stand! A press release had been sent to local media prior to the event, and the coverage was enough to launch a successful retail business.

THE BUSINESS OF AWARDS

What I have been describing is basically the same principle that governs all show business awards, from the Emmys to the Tonys to the Academy Awards. Each of those award ceremonies was originally created to sell stars and their products. The recipients stand to make millions of dollars by being selected for awards. Of course, over the years, the ceremonies themselves have become such media events that the awards generate millions of dollars in advertising revenues for their sponsors and broadcasters.

Virtually every industry has an awards banquet. Whether for advertising agencies or fashion houses, publishing companies or police departments, awards awaken the public to their merits and generate either sales or good will, or both.

If, however, you are in neither a glamorous business (e.g., moviemaking) nor an exciting line of work (e.g., cops and firemen), you will have to figure out a way of generating awards that will capture public attention, as I did with the aforementioned pet store.

FITNESS AWARDS

Let me give you one more example of what can be done to generate public acclamation via awards. As I related in Chapter 1, I once owned and operated a day camp in Bridgehampton, New York. I decided to train all of my campers to pass. the test for the President's

Council on Physical Fitness and Sports It was, in some ways, a grueling test, but one that most kids could pass if they were not too young, especially if they were trained to do so. Every day for an hour, I trained my campers in various fitness routines. After several weeks, I felt that they were all fit to pass the test. I had even gotten one rather fat and sedentary little boy into sufficiently good shape so that he, too, could pass the test. When the appropriate day arrived, I administered the test, and each of my campers passed, including the fat little boy. Indeed, his passing the test probably did more to improve his self-image and self-confidence than anything else he had previously done. The following year, he had transformed into a trim young athlete.

After the test was completed, I sent the results to Washington, and each student received a special award from President Ford. My former partner and I also went to Washington, where we received awards for our accomplishments. We each received a Presidential Sports Fitness Pin with the seal of the United States on it.

Next, we had an awards ceremony attended by parents and local media. One newspaper reported that our day camp had not only helped more children to pass the President's Fitness Test than any other camp, but that our campers were the youngest kids in the country to pass such a test. We had not only been honored and had our accomplishments certified in the media, but we had also become experts. As a result, parents couldn't wait to send their children to us.

We topped it all off by taking out a large newspaper advertisement in which we noted our accomplishments and reprinted the Presidential awards. It almost looked as if the president himself had taken out the ad to congratulate us and to urge others on to achieve similar goals.

There are probably athletic competitions that your small business could sponsor and for which you could give awards. The resulting publicity would serve to generate a considerable amount of good will, while also raising awareness of your business. You could sponsor anything from a baseball, basketball, or football team of young athletes to a group of joggers, hikers, or bicyclists.

TO TELL THE TRUTH

Unfortunately, there are many promoters who have less than a deep-seated admiration for the truth. For example, I recall reading recently that a press agent for Rita Hayworth once named her the winner of a nonexistent beauty contest. As a result of the ensuing newspaper coverage, she got her first starring role in a Hollywood film.

I mention that because the same principle of self-promotion governs many different businesses ventures. What's difficult is finding the kind of self-promoting awards that will increase your profits.

Years ago, I knew a young criminal defense lawyer who decided he needed publicity to build his practice. He had handled a number of cases, none of which had gotten him any public notice. One day, he decided to invite all the defendants for whom he had won acquittals to a dinner in his honor in Chinatown. He told each of the ten diners that he was giving himself an award for keeping innocent men from going to jail. He chose a cheap restaurant with several long tables, so that all of his guests could sit at one table, and their meals would not cost him a small fortune, which is what he was trying to accumulate. He bought himself a bronzed ball-and-chain mounted on a fake slab of mahogany. He had a photographer take a picture of the presentation of the award. No newspapers attended his little ceremony, so he wrote his own newspaper article and had it reproduced with the photograph. It was all done in the style of one of the city's more notorious tabloids. He even invented a headline, something to the effect of "Lawyer Keeps Criminals Safe From New York."

Thereafter, he sent copies of the faux article, along with his business card, to people of means who were arrested for a variety of crimes. Having achieved a modicum of success, he still hadn't accumulated a small fortune, so he later became a lawyer/manager for a number of celebrities whom, he felt, appreciated him more than the criminal classes had. In addition, they had more money.

I don't advise you to try such things, for if the media ever learns the truth, it will publicize the fact that you have attempted to hood-wink people, and your once-good reputation will sink like a stone tossed into a lake.

WHAT NOT TO DO

There are plenty of people who will even make up testimonials, and then attribute them to people who have never set eyes on them.

When I was in college, I spent a summer working in stock theater. The owner of the stock company was one of those theatrical eccentrics who had enjoyed moderate success in the 1940s, after which his career had leveled off, then precipitously declined. By the time he hired me as a stage manager, he was hustling every angle for a buck. In addition to such strategies as not signing checks, writing two different amounts on the same check, and sending the wrong checks to creditors, he scrounged deals with cheap restaurants and boardinghouse owners for himself and his employees. At the end of every summer, a number of semi- or former stars who had consented to appear in his productions always sued him for salaries he had failed to pay.

During the summer season, he decided that he required the testimonials of famous men and women who could bring in large audiences to see his plays. In addition to raves from critics such as George Bernard Shaw and H.L. Mencken, who had been dead for a while, he also quoted well-known living critics from prestigious newspapers and magazines. When I asked him how he could manufacture rave comments from people who had never seen his productions, he simply said: "It's easy. I used to write play reviews when I was in college, so I know how to do it."

"No," I explained, "I mean, how can you get away with making things up?"

"The critics that I quote will never come here, so they will never know they are being quoted. In fact, they are really doing many good deeds, for they are keeping actors, who wouldn't otherwise work, employed. In fact, without those rave reviews, you wouldn't have a job for the summer. Think of that!" he said and sauntered off for an afternoon nap.

The following summer, one of my former colleagues told me that the intrepid theatrical impresario had been threatened with a lawsuit from a newspaper and its leading theatrical critic, if he didn't cease and desist. He then substituted another name for that of the litigious critic.

Such theft of another's name, of course, goes beyond the bounds of what anyone can rightly do. I offer it merely as an example of how far someone, even a charming rascal, can get the testimonials of people who enjoy the respect of the community.

On a more mundane level, let me conclude this chapter with an example of a set of ads that helped dramatically increase business for a brokerage firm. A man I knew had a number of celebrities give genuine testimonials to the firm for helping them to become rich. The firm benefited enormously from the testimonials, which were seen on television and heard on radio. No one, however, noted that the brokerage firm further helped to enrich those celebrities by paying them for their testimonials.

QUICK TIPS FOR SUCCESS

If your business is going to succeed, you must continuously promote your accomplishments to prospects who will subsequently become your customer or clients.

You can do this through press releases, brochures, newsletters, direct mail packages, personalized letters, and phone calls.

In addition, you should take advantage of testimonials and awards as ways of furthering people's knowledge, admiration, and appreciation of your services/products.

Keep in mind the formula that you should spend 50% of your time generating new business and 50% of your time servicing existing business.

Your greatest award will be your own success, a testimonial to your diligence and creativity.

CHAPTER 6

Organizing
Special Events

Millions of people love a circus, a carnival, a parade. If your business could be such an event, just imagine the success that would follow! For clients with limited budgets, I have regularly sought to organize special events that would generate both good will and increased profits.

A special event occurs infrequently and arouses public interest as well as that of the media. Many special events are scripted by clever marketing and promotion professionals; others may be spontaneous, but still may be taken advantage of to promote a product/service.

For example, when the Ringling Brothers, Barnum & Bailey Circus parades its elephants through the Midtown Tunnel into Manhattan, it receives a considerable amount of newspaper and television news coverage. After all, how often do long lines of elephants trod through a major tunnel into the world's foremost city? If, however, the elephants were to become panicked and stampede through the tunnel, erupting onto the streets of New York City, where they turned over cars and trampled pedestrians, the ensuing publicity would be infinitely greater than the amount resulting from a placid, pleasant parade through the tunnel. And just imagine, for a moment, the number of curiosity seekers who would buy tickets to the circus just to see the wild elephants.

The former is a mild staged event that is entirely controlled; the latter is a spontaneous one. Both afford marketers the opportunity to sell tickets.

You will rarely, if ever, have the opportunity to benefit from natural disasters; but, if you do, this chapter will teach you how. More importantly, however, it will give you examples of carefully scripted and staged special events that can have positive marketing results for your business.

STAGING SPECIAL EVENTS

Before moving on to staged special events, I shall give you an example of a spontaneous event that can benefit an organization, while—unfortunately—causing significant turmoil in the lives of many people.

Every time there is a hurricane or earthquake, donations to the American Red Cross shoot way up. If there were no natural disasters, the Red Cross would have a difficult time generating donations. It is a sorry, but true, situation in which an important philanthropic organization depends on public misery for its success. There are many other well-meaning organizations that similarly benefit from unfortunate events.

Unless you want to be arrested, you should not attempt to stage a natural disaster. Besides, there are already too many. You can, however, use such a disaster to benefit the victims, while also promoting your own business. More often, however, you will have the opportunity to create public special events that are charming, enjoyable, and entertaining. Such events, while rarely causing a catharsis, will nevertheless inspire people to respond positively to your products/services.

COATS FOR KIDS

Here is an example of confronting a natural disaster of sorts by helping many unfortunate children, while reaping significant and well-deserved benefits.

A number of years ago, I represented the Neighborhood Cleaners' Association (N.C.A.), a trade association that represents more than 4,000 dry cleaners in about 10 states. The organization is devoted to high professional standards and customer satisfaction. It also operates a dry-cleaning school, and regularly issues consumer bulletins about which garments can and cannot be successfully cleaned, warning consumers not to purchase those garments which are shoddily manufactured and cannot be successfully dry cleaned.

Nearly all dry cleaners are left with garments that no one wants. For example, a mother brings in her son's winter coat at the end of the winter season. She asks for it to be cleaned. Her son then grows a couple of inches, and winter has turned to spring. She forgets about the coat, no longer needs it. Why spend money to clean a garment that is too small to be worn? She leaves the coat with her neighborhood dry cleaners.

Multiply that situation by hundreds of thousands of people in hundred of cities! Dry cleaners, like other store owners, have a limited amount of floor space. If they turn their valuable space into storage space, they will surely lose money.

Working with the executive director of the N.C.A., Bill Seitz, we decided that rather than throwing those coats away (which had technically become the property of the dry cleaners), we would donate the coats to kids whose parents could not afford to buy them new winter coats.

111

We made an arrangement with the Salvation Army to pick up and distribute winter coats. The coats would be given to homeless kids in shelters and kids in welfare hotels. I then wrote a press release about the event, and secured numerous public service announcements on radio and television. In fact, I even appeared on a WABC-TV public service spot that aired several times a day for a full week.

Dry cleaners put up posters in their stores, asking customers to bring in kids' coats that they no longer wanted, to be donated to kids who didn't have winter coats.

The program, called Coats for Kids, became so popular that in subsequent years, companies all across America joined. Now it is a national endeavor in which everyone wants to participate. Its success is enormous. Not only do many thousands of kids get warm winter coats, but thousands of companies get the opportunity to do good *and* raise public appreciation of their mercantile endeavors. For local dry cleaners, the positive publicity has been extraordinary.

TURNING A PROFIT WHILE DOING GOOD

Raising money (or giving away valuable merchandise) for charitable purposes has always been a sure-fire way of garnering public esteem, and that esteem can be turned into dollars. After all, there is nothing wrong with turning a profit while also doing good. In fact, it is an excellent incentive.

Here is another example of doing good while raising much-needed funds for an important charity. In 1984, I was hired to publicize an event for the Kidney Foundation of New York. The Foundation had decided to put on a nostalgia concert with a local radio station, WNEW-AM—the station was celebrating its 50th anniversary. For years, it had been the major outlet for pop songs from the 1930s, 40s, and 50s, playing the music of Frank Sinatra, Vic Damone, Peggy Lee, Billie Holiday, Ella Fitzgerald,

Eddie Fisher, Doris Day, Dean Martin, Bing Crosby, Tony Bennett, Sammy Davis, Jr., Woody Herman, Benny Goodman, the Andrew Sisters, Nat King Cole, etc. The station's disc jockeys were themselves local celebrities; in fact, Frank Sinatra regularly referred to one of them, William B. Williams, as the "Chairman of the Board."

The Kidney Foundation's concert was to be held at Madison Square Garden; the entertainers would be some of those previously noted, with the disc jockeys as masters of ceremonies.

How to publicize such an event? If I could have gotten the entertainers to appear on television and radio, I would have had no trouble. They were not available to publicize the event, however.

The disc jockeys were another story; after all, their radio station would benefit from the publicity and the concert, dramatically increasing the number of their listeners. I began by preparing several press releases that were sent to newspapers and magazines, all of whom ran stories about the upcoming event. I needed something more. I called one of the disc jockeys, Jim Lowe, and asked if he and others would be available to appear on television interview programs. Of course, he agreed. I quickly booked him and the others on all the 5:00 P.M. local television news shows. I also booked them on local morning television shows that aired at 9:00 A.M. and 10:00 A.M.

The concert proved an enormous success. Every seat in Madison Square Garden had been sold; the Kidney Foundation raised much-needed funds; and WNEW generated new interest in its station and its music, especially among younger listeners who hadn't previously been part of their audience.

MUSIC TO THE EARS OF CUSTOMERS

While the Kidney Foundation concert involved well-known entertainers and raised a considerable amount of money, there are less formidable events that can help small businesses.

When I owned and operated my gymnastics school in New York

City, for example, I wanted to spread the word about how effective we were in training competitive gymnasts. The mother of one of our young gymnasts was a music teacher at an inner-city school in the Bronx. She led a symphony orchestra there, made up of students who loved music. They played classical music, jazz, popular tunes, and big band music from the 1930s.

I made arrangements with a junior high school in Manhattan, near my gymnastics school, to rent its auditorium. The orchestra from the Bronx would provide the musical accompaniment to choreographed gymnastics routines. We decided to sell tickets to the event, and to donate the money to a charity that helped learning-disabled children.

I sent out press releases announcing the event; then I wrote to celebrities who lived on the Upper West Side of Manhattan. I asked them to attend the recital as my guest; or if they could not, then perhaps they would publicly announce that we were doing something worthwhile that the community at large should support. A number of local politicians and celebrities did, in fact, offer to help. One of those who was unable to attend but who complimented us for putting together such an event was the world-renowned composer and conductor, Leonard Bernstein.

On the evening of the event, all the kids were nervous, and their parents were excited. No one, including my partner and myself, had any idea that so many people would turn out to see preteens and teenagers perform gymnastics routines, and to hear an orchestra from an inner-city high school. Both the gymnasts and the musicians performed with skill and enthusiasm; indeed, theirs was the kind of open-hearted enthusiasm that is so infectiously and wonderfully characteristic of youth.

Two local television news programs attended, and used filmed clips to conclude their news shows at 11:00 P.M. In addition, we raised several thousand dollars that was donated to a charity, and the good will generated by the event caused our enrollment to shoot up.

SPECIAL EVENTS FOR STORES

Even an enterprise as small as a single store can put on an effective special event that will produce positive results. I concocted such an event, which produced a dramatic increase in sales for a sports store that sold ski equipment in the winter. To promote the store and its equipment, I arranged for the New York City Parks Department to let me use Central Park to prepare people for ski weekends, so that they would be less likely get injured on the slopes. I had a fitness instructor lead a group of ski enthusiasts in a series of pre-ski exercises in the park. The sports store supplied all the equipment, as well as a large sign that was placed on an easel. Several dozen people showed up for the event, as did several television news programs. I had alerted them to the event by sending out a press release and a media alert. (A "media alert" answers the questions who, why, when, where, what, and how. It is a series of six short paragraphs, each no longer than a single sentence.) The sign with my client's name was clearly visible in all the news coverage of people exercising on their skis.

Each of the participants received a coupon for 10% off the purchase of ski equipment a my client's store; sales jumped dramatically. For several years thereafter, the sports store not only put on "Get-in-Shape for Skiing" classes at the park, but also sponsored such classes at other gyms, where it loaned equipment for the classes and provided discount coupons for subsequent purchase.

TAPPING INTO ANOTHER SPECIAL EVENT

An alternative to putting on your own special event is to tap into another event—one not of your own making, yet one that will benefit you. For example, one of my clients had a flower business that specialized in weddings. I learned that another client was going to be the best man at a nudist wedding ceremony in Pennsylvania. I asked him if it would be all right for me to call the bride and groom.

115

I wanted to find out if my client could supply the bridal bouquet and any other flowers that would be needed.

He called the soon-to-be-married couple, and told them about my request. He asked if I could call; they agreed. After a few polite words, I got to the subject, and they agreed that my client could supply the bridal bouquet and altar flowers, if she could deliver them for 10% less than another florist with whom they had been speaking. My client said that she could.

I wrote a press release announcing that my client was supplying flowers to a nudist wedding. The media loved the idea; though the nudist couple did not want media coverage of their wedding, they did give several interviews to newspapers, and permitted their photos to be taken from the neck up. It was, indeed, a special event, one that significantly benefited my client's business!

I found another event that the same client could tap into, and from which she could reap significant benefits: a huge AIDS benefit in New York City that would receive enormous news coverage. There would be a dinner, a dance, and an auction, and all the money would go to help find a cure for AIDS. Each of the guests at the event would receive a program; in that program would be ads for people who wanted to have their products/services connected with a worthwhile cause. I arranged for my client to donate all the flowers for the night's festivities. In exchange for her donation, she received a free full-page advertisement in the program, as well as letters of gratitude from the event's organizers.

Altogether, as you might have imagined, her participation in the event brought her many new customers. Because the fight against AIDS is one of the most vigorous being conducted against any disease at present, I have urged my clients to do good while reaping obvious benefits.

Here is another example of a small business being able to take advantage of special events. A client has a jewelry business that designs, manufactures, and sells fine jewelry; he also sells wholesale diamonds. Through Gay Men's Health Crisis (GMHC), I arranged for him to create a beautiful pin made of gold, platinum, and diamonds. It would be auctioned at one of New York's premier art galleries, and all the proceeds would go to GMHC. The pin had a value of $10,000. Following the auction, my client had not only established himself as an important beneficiary of a worthy cause, but he could also say that he was one of the few jewelers in the world who had created a pin that was auctioned at an important New York gallery. What a coup!

That same fellow had come to New York from Russia a little more than ten years before, and had sold peanuts from a stand on Fifth Avenue in front of the Empire State Building. Now, his business grosses more than $3.5 million a year, and he employs eleven people. Only in America, as some pundit once said.

HOW TO PREPARE FOR A SPECIAL EVENT

If you are going to benefit from participating in a special event, you should begin to prepare as early as possible. Typically, special events are planned at least six months in advance. Call local charities and ask what events they will be putting on over the next twelve months. The larger charitable organizations usually have someone on staff whose sole responsibility is to put on special events.

Once you find a charity and an upcoming event to which you think you can contribute products or services, set up a meeting with the organization. Write a plan of what you can do that will benefit the charity, but that will also have positive ramifications for your business as well. Charities, to be blunt, are always looking for "freebies"; however, if you simply donate a product or service, you may merely be one of many good samaritans. Such people become nearly anonymous in the overall event. To prevent that from happening to you, be sure that your product/service is absolutely integral to the success of the event. In other words, when the executive director of the charity thanks you for your contributions and says they could not have done it without you, make sure he's telling the truth. And make sure that others will know about it too! Your contributions can easily be overlooked, either because charities have so much else to be concerned about, or because you are simply being taken for granted.

If you are to avoid being a nonentity, then the events must either be controlled by you, or you must be able to get your story to the media independently of the charity's efforts.

RECREATIONAL MATH

For example, I recently donated "Math Made Easy" tutorial videotapes to the city of New York. A client of mine manufactures and distributes these highly successful tapes, and has recently formed a nonprofit foundation to help educate underprivileged children. The tapes will be used by the city in after-school recreational programs to help children from kindergarten through high school become proficient in all aspects of mathematics. In addition, my client has created a preschool reading videotape called "Reading Is Easy," which also was donated to the city.

While we were happy to provide free tapes for such a good cause, we also wanted to get as much publicity for the gift as possible. Therefore, I told the contact person at the after-school program that we would make a gift of the tapes only if the city would set up a special event, a ceremony honoring my client for their good deeds. The city, eager to have the tapes, agreed. We got the publicity that I had insisted upon, and I also sent out my own press release with a photo of the event.

ROCK 'N' ROLL MOVIE LOSES MONEY, MAKES MONEY

Events are not always as easy as that to create. I once had a client who made a movie about rock 'n' roll; it was an amateurish film that could not possibly earn back its original investment. There was no way that we could get movie reviewers to praise the movie, though many of them had praised well-financed productions that were far worse than my client's.

The only way the movie could make any money would be if it was used as a fund-raising vehicle for charities. We would rent the movie inexpensively to charities, who could then show it to nostalgia buffs interested in music from the 1950s. The idea worked; various charities rented the movie and used it to raise funds.

My client did not make a lot of money, though he eventually broke even and paid off those who had loaned money for the movie's production. He did, however, make a name for himself, and he now has a company that creates infomercials (which—in a way—was what his first movie proved to be).

VIDEO GAME TOURNAMENTS

Here is another example of how a special event can have a positive marketing effect.

In 1981, I worked for a company that was given the assignment of promoting video games. Such games were very popular at the time, and many companies were trying to sell their products to eager teenagers.

Our client had a product called Intellevision. One could play games of skill against others as well as against the clock. With so many companies offering video games, it was difffficult—but not impossible—to set oneself apart from the herd. We decided to put on video game tournaments in the biggest markets around the country. Exhibit 6-1 shows a newspaper article announcing one of these events.

We secured great locations for our tournaments, such as the lobby of the World Trade Center. In each location, we set up more than 100 televisions and video games, and invited all comers to participate. The tournaments lasted from 9:00 A.M. to 1:00 P.M. The winners received cash prizes as well as free video games and other related merchandise. The arrangement of 100 screens and thou-

EXHIBIT 6-1 Special events can have a positive marketing effect. Here, a newspaper article announces a video game tournament that was arranged as a promotional event for a new product called Intellevision.

——Hot Flashes!——

If you're not into video games, stay away from the King of Prussia Mall Saturday. That's when Gino's and the folks who make Mattel's Intellivision video system are expecting 1,500 people to participate in a video competition with more than $10,000 in prizes for the winners.

Jeff Sussman of TRG Communications says all 1,500 competitors will test their skill on the "Downhill Skiing" game. Then, the top 50 scorers will compete on "Auto Racing," with just two finalists battling it out on Mattel's "Baseball."

First prize is an Intellivision game with 25 game cartridges *and* a giant screen RCA projection TV. To enter, pick up an entry blank at participating Gino's or show up at the contest site, King of Prussia Mall, lower level, adjacent to John Wanamakers at 10 a.m.

☆   ☆   ☆

Burt Reynolds appears to be the No. 1 hero of eighth grade America. The World Almanac & Book of Facts (NEA-Ballantine, $4.50) polled 2,000 eighth graders on the 30 people they most admired and wanted to be like when they grew up. Reynolds, 45, came in first for the second year in a row.

All but three of the 30 were entertainers. The three exceptions were sports figures **"Sugar" Ray Leonard**, **"Magic" Johnson** and **Earl Campbell**. No politicians were named. The oldest winner was **George Burns**, 85. The youngest was Brooke Shields, 16, who also was the top ranking female. The top 10 were: Reynolds, **Richard Pryor, Alan Alda**, Shields, **John Ritter**, Scott Baio, Bo Derek, Burns, Leonard and **Steve Martin**.

☆   ☆   ☆

Think you're alone in your love for toy trains — an affection that somehow seems to blossom at this time every year. You're not.

Reynolds

Toy trains, which have been around since 1900, were never more popular than they are today — according to the December issue of Town & Country, with collectors that include **Frank Sinatra, Roy Rogers, Tom Snyder** and Virginia Sen. **John Warner, Elizabeth Taylor's** husband. The toy railroad boom began in the 1940s and '50s, when about 500,000 permanently set up Lionel layouts carried many times more engines and boxcars than the rolling stock of full-sized U.S. railroads.

☆   ☆   ☆

Margaret Trudeau, estranged wife of Canadian Prime Minister **Pierre Trudeau**, is finishing up her new book. It's the sequel to "Beyond Reason," Maggie's 1979 autobiography. This one's to be dubbed "Consequences." The topic: her life since her last book. With the task of writing an autobiography every three years, we wonder when the lady has time to do the things she writes about.

☆   ☆   ☆

Last time we caught a glimpse of **Rita Jenrette** in Playboy, so entranced were we by her, ah, natural attributes that we forgot what else was in the photos. But in the December issue of **Hugh Hefner's** favorite mag we find a photo of a lovely Rita, fully clothed and phoning in a story to her People Paper editors. (Rita, remember,

Trudeau

covered the Miss America Pageant for the Daily News.) And right beside Rita the reporter is our favorite page in the whole paper — and yours too, we hope.

sands of teenagers who wanted to participate naturally drew the television news programs, as well as photographers from newspapers and magazines. It was a visual bonanza! I also had an enormous banner strung across the area; it proclaimed INTELLEVISION. We also had a raffle in each location, so that several lucky people would receive free video games. Parents and children came to the events just to take advantage of the free raffle.

I recall one Sunday morning in New York. I had arranged for media coverage of the video game tournament at the World Trade Center. I got a call that morning from a national correspondent for a network news show. I met him at Grand Central Terminal, and we took a subway downtown. He was not happy, for he was a serious journalist who wanted to cover the important events of the day, and here he was about to cover a frothy video game event. His wonderful story appeared on the national news that night, and my client could not have been happier. He figured that the network news coverage was worth a million dollars, not only in sales of Intellevision, but also in sales of other products, as well as ancillary rights. The reporter went on to become a significant presence on network news, and I doubt he would even condescend to cover such stories now. There are, however, plenty of other journalists who enjoy such media events simply because many of them are lots of fun!

REVERSE STRIPTEASE

Speaking of fun, one of the first special events that I put on generated a lot of smiles on the faces of news photographers. Shortly after graduating from college, I was working for a public relations agency that primarily handled rock singers. (Looking back, I realize that we were better at getting them publicity than at helping them live long, happy lives—our clients included Jimi Hendrix and Janis Joplin, among others who are now either dead or forgotten.) One of our clients at the time, however, was not in the music business. It was a trade show at the New York Coliseum, designed to promote winter sports and all of the accoutrements that went along with such sports. It was to be held for one week in the middle of February, when the thermometer would dip into the low teens. It was also at a time when the so-called sexual revolution was on the minds and libidos of many New Yorkers, and the women's movement was just an inkling (I say all of this by way of a defense).

I was given the assignment of getting publicity for the event and, being a New Yorker of his time, I realized that sex would get us coverage. I ran an ad in a theatrical trade paper asking for models and/or actresses who were willing to pose in their underwear. They would promote a winter sports festival. I promised not only to pay them, but to provide valuable publicity that could possibly benefit their careers.

A number of absolutely beautiful young women responded to the ad. Most had what (I gather) are called "full-bodied" figures. I asked them if they minded appearing in their underwear on the streets of New York. They all agreed to perform in my scenario.

I next contacted the media, letting them know that there would be a striptease on the streets of New York, right in front of the Coliseum. I hired a rock band (though not a famous one) to provide the accompanying music necessary for bumps and grinds. About eight photographers from local newspapers showed up, as did three television and two radio news reporters.

I assembled them around a small platform that had been constructed for the event. The band, off to one side, began playing a hard-driving drum beat accompanied by a sexually suggestive saxophone. It drew dozens of spectators.

"Where are the girls?" shouted one grizzled old photographer, the kind of guy who would probably have been wearing a rain coat in a darkened porno theater.

"They'll be out in a minute," I said.

Next, I placed a pile of ski clothing on the platform; there were six different outfits in six different piles.

I went to a microphone in front of the platform and announced: "Now, you will witness the first-ever reverse striptease. Six comely females will shortly appear in their underwear, and put on the ski clothes you see on the platform. The one who does it most erotically will be named Miss Winter Sports Queen, and receive a prize of $100 worth of free merchandise."

The band struck up a new song—as if a champion football team had run out onto a field to be welcomed by tens of thousands of enthusiastic fans. Each young woman was wearing a brightly colored bra and panties; they had little time to get dressed before the New York winter cold would cause their flesh to be covered by goosebumps. They dressed quickly, yet were surprisingly graceful and sexy. The band played, the photographers shot photos.

The young women were soon warm, and pleased to be the center of so much attention. While none of them, as far as I know, went on to become famous, the show at the Coliseum received all of the publicity for which the promoters had wished; it was well attended, and they handsomely profited from the event.

QUICK TIPS FOR SUCCESS

I could describe other special events, but you should come up with your own. I believe that all of the examples I have provided will help you to dream up special events for your own business ventures. If you need additional inspiration, look through local newspapers and carefully watch local television news programs. You will see it all with fresh eyes and, I'm sure, get many good ideas that will benefit your business. Good luck.

CHAPTER 7

Signs For Success,
Signs Of The Times

When I was a little boy and decided to sell lemonade from a roadside stand, I made a sign even before I asked my mother to help me mix the lemonade. Already at age four, I realized it was more important to know how to market a product than to have the product ready for the market. Having seen signs for lemonade in comic books, I made a large sign on a piece of oaktag. It read: "Lemonade—25 Cents." Of course, I crossed out the "25 Cents" and substituted a new price of "10 Cents." I also added the following explanation: "Today only. Special sale!" It worked: I sold out my entire supply of lemonade. I invested my considerable profits in packet after packet of new baseball cards.

Ever since that first great success, I have not only been aware of the power of signs, but I have always been fascinated by unusual and often garish signs. Prior to the age of television, roadside signs were a popular way of advertising virtually every consumer commodity in America. While newspapers, magazines, and television are often too expensive for most small businesses, there are a host of less expensive signs that are highly effective marketing tools.

SCANTILY CLAD WITH SIGNS

Following in the successful tradition of Lady Godiva (who rode naked upon a horse), I helped a friend open a new restaurant in Manhattan in the late 1960s. We hired twelve not-quite-topless dancers to ride bicycles through various nearby neighborhoods. The women were as close to naked as they legally were able to be; they all carried signs, some of which were banners that were hung between two bicycles. Each sign announced the opening of the restaurant (which, by the way, was not topless).

As crowds gathered along the sidewalks to witness the parade of beautiful, nearly naked bicyclists, two women from the rear of the procession handed out discount coupons that offered two regular entrees for the price of one. Coffee, desserts, and alcoholic beverages were not included.

PICKETERS IN BIKINIS

This promotion proved so successful that I worked a variation on that theme to open another restaurant. I hired eight very tall, beautiful models. Each wore a bikini and carried a picket sign. Some of the signs proclaimed that the proprietor of the restaurant that they were picketing was a wonderful man, kind, generous, and sensitive. Others claimed that the food inside was the best possible food they had ever eaten, and the prices were amazingly reasonable.

Not only did our bikini-clad models draw in many customers, but the media found the event entertaining. I had alerted local television news programs, and several of them sent camera crews. They were not only charmed by the picketers in bikinis, but they were amused by the signs praising a restaurant that was ostensibly being "picketed." You should keep in mind that though the women carried signs, they were perceived as signs of a different kind: the signs had positive, rather than negative, messages.

EFFECTIVE SIGNS

If it would be impossible or inappropriate for you to hire beautiful models, then your signage must be extremely effective. In most cases, for a sign to attract attention and to effect stronger sales, it should offer something that is either free or on sale. An effective way of offering a freebie is the common practice of "buy one, get one free." The words "free" and "sale" have been tested and proven, time after time, to be particularly effective in all kinds of signs.

For example, focus groups have proven that certain words and phrases generate positive responses from potential consumers: "free," "sale," "new," "sex," "love," "dollars," "millions of dollars," and "long life." Focus groups have also proven that the most effective signs have the fewest number of words, no polysyllabic words, no grandiloquent sesquipedalian sentences. In addition, signs should stand out, and differ from nearby signs. Thus, if you are putting up a sign in a garden of colorful signs, you may want one that is just black and white. Conversely, if you want to advertise in a graveyard of dull, dreary signs, then create a sign that is a dazzling array of colors. Interesting examples are the occasional black-and-white television commercials which appear in otherwise full-color programs.

In addition to color, punctuation is an extremely important consideration. You should always keep punctuation to a minimum in signs. Everything that you learned in high school grammar should be ignored. The most effective punctuation in a sign is an exclamation mark! Avoid commas, semi-colons, and colons whenever possible.

127

CREATIVE USE OF SIGNS

There is perhaps no better way to learn than from experience. Many years after my success as a big-time operator of a roadside lemonade stand, I opened an art gallery in Lenox, Massachusetts. I was a New York University student at the time, and I wanted to escape the City's hot, humid summers. My gallery was in an old barn, set back about 400 feet from an infrequently traveled road. Rather than calling it the Da Vinci Art Gallery or the Rembrandt Fine Arts Emporium, I decided that the name of my gallery should indicate something about its location. Hence, I called it The Needle in the Haystack Art Gallery. I printed about 100 extremely colorful signs with the name, address, and phone number of the gallery. Since finding the gallery was a little easier than actually finding a needle in a haystack, I decided to create weekly treasure hunts with clues strewn through the town of Lenox. I got merchants to put up signs stating that they were participating in our treasure hunt, which generated business traffic for them. Each of the gallery signs also stated that we had weekly treasure hunts, and the treasure was a small work of art. I had turned a visit to my gallery into a small but enjoyable adventure, not only for local residents, but also for summer tourists. I had taken an out-of-the-way location and, through the use of a name and effective signage, turned it to my advantage.

At the time, I owned an unusual-looking car; it was a Citroen Deux Cheveaux, which many people called a tunafish can on four wheels. I had the car painted to resemble a black-and-white leopard. On each side of the car, I attached large signs for my art gallery. The signs were bright red and had shiny white lettering. Every day, I drove through not just Lenox, but the surrounding towns as well. I would stop the car at corners where large numbers of tourists were waiting to cross the streets. I handed each one a flyer for the gallery and told them about the treasure hunt.

I had several hundred bumper stickers printed with the name of the art gallery and its phone number. I asked people if I could put stickers on their bumpers; about 60% said no, they didn't want to advertise my gallery. I offered each one a dollar to rent advertising space on their bumpers for the summer; nearly all agreed. I not only gladly paid the dollars, but I regularly invited each of my advertisers to attend weekly gallery openings, where jug wine and pretzels were served. It was wonderful to see all the cars driving up with the name of my gallery on their bumpers. I also arranged for a company to print a color photo of my gallery on T-shirts. I sold the T-shirts, donating all the profits to a camp for children with learning disabilities. Customers were pleased to support such a camp, and they helped me by wearing T-shirts that advertised my art gallery. Similar to the concept of the scantily clad models, they became walking signs too!

So successful did I make the Needle in the Hay Stack Art Gallery that I was able to spend cool summers out of the hot city and in the delightful Berkshire Mountains. If it hadn't been for the creative use of signs, I would have been sitting in a damp barn reading one book after another. I would have returned to New York in debt, rather than with money in my pocket.

GUERRILLA POSTERERS

Here is another example of how effective signs can be in creating success for a different sort of venture. I regularly attend musical concerts, and have enjoyed helping producers of such concerts to be successful. A producer that I know called me one night, and asked if I would promote a concert at a nearby church. The church would be hosting a European choral group that would perform Mozart's Requiem.

Naturally, I sent out press releases announcing the concert, and the information was printed in weekly and daily newspapers. In addition, two classical music radio stations announced the concert several times a day for a week. As effective as all that would be, it would not be sufficient to sell every seat for the concert.

While in college, I had heard of a group of former hippies who had organized a company called the Midnight Posterers. For several hundred dollars, an army of them would swoop through the city, pasting signs to utility poles, boarded-up buildings, and construction sites that were ringed by boards nailed together to keep pedestrians out.

A printer who was a member of the church's congregation created 1,200 signs, at cost. I could not locate the Midnight Posterers, for they were like guerrillas, and did not advertise in the Yellow Pages; however, I was able to track down a similar group. In the course of one long night, they papered every kind of pole and wall in the borough of Manhattan that the law permitted.

THUMB-TACK SOLDIERS

I asked my posterers if they knew of another group that would tack up smaller signs on bulletin boards throughout Manhattan. They recommended a group of thumbtack soldiers. I created a series of smaller signs, ranging in size from 3 × 5 to 5 × 7 inches. The thumbtack soldiers tacked these little signs on thousands of bulletin boards, from those in church basements to laundromats to schools to community centers to police stations.

The church not only sold tickets for every seat, but they also sold additional tickets for standing room at 65% off. The church earned more than $25,000 for its annual music program!

I have used simple but effective signs for a wide variety of other businesses, including a flower shop, a hair-styling salon, a nail salon, an astrologist, a psychiatrist, a banjo teacher, a strip-o-gram company, an accountant, and a trio of juggling dwarfs.

POINT-OF-PURCHASE SIGNS

Another kind of sign that is extremely important is the P-O-P or point-of-purchase sign. It is one of the most effective marketing tools for retailers and for those who sell their products to retailers.

Such signs are usually found near the cashier, and alert the consumer to the availability of merchandise that is within arm's reach.

In many cases, however, the signs do not need to be near the cashier; the signs can be near one kind of product that you will buy, while alerting you to another related product.

For example, if you buy a jar of peanut butter in a supermarket, there may be a sign on the shelf alerting you to a special price offer on bread and/or jelly. If you are a student about to purchase a notebook, you may see a sign for pens. Such signs frequently offer a discount if you buy more than one product.

I was recently in a drugstore. At the cashier's counter, there were stacks of cough drops. Nearby was a sign that offered nasal sprays. If you bought both products from the same manufacturer, you would benefit from a 15% discount

There are also P-O-P signs for restaurants. Several years ago, I helped a young couple introduce a special "veggie burger" into coffee shops. In order to get the owners of the coffee shops to take the veggie burgers, we offered them tent cards, which are double-sided ads in the shape of pup tents: two upright and angled panels have printed ads, while the bottom panel supports the other two.

Many of the coffee-shop owners we had solicited agreed to order the veggie burgers if we supplied attractive four-color tent cards that advertised the product. We were delighted, because it gave us an opportunity to advertise the burgers. No other food products were being advertised on the tables, so we enjoyed a significant advantage. And, quite obviously, if a hungry diner goes into a coffee shop and sees a mouth-watering photo of a delicious veggie burger on a bun with lettuce and tomatoes and French fries, that diner will eagerly contemplate that burger before anything else on the menu!

Point-of-purchase signs are, indeed, highly effective selling agents, offering valuable product information. Furthermore, P-O-P signs can inspire a sale by offering premiums, discounts, and coupons.

When one of my clients, a small stationery store, needed to boost sales, I contacted the manufacturers of virtually all of the products in the store. I asked for any P-O-P signs that they had. Without exception, they all responded positively, and we placed P-O-P signs throughout the store. Near notebooks, we placed signs for paper, pens, and briefcases. Near briefcases, we placed signs for notebooks, paper, and pens. In other words, it was a matter of many two-way streets, each item with its P-O-P signs selling related items.

ARTICLES INTO SIGNS

Signs can also be reproduced from other marketing tools. For example, one of my clients recently benefited from an excellent story in a prestigious New York magazine. The story brought his jewelry store a considerable amount of new business. For all those, however, who did not see the story, or needed to be reminded of it, I made two three-foot-high posters of the article. I placed one in the window, and the other inside the store. The presence of those two signs dramatically increased his business for an additional month.

OTHER SIGN POSSIBILITIES

Manufacturers, incidentally, will often provide you with large signs featuring their products. You can print the name of your store on their sign, and use it to market their products.

Speaking of unusual places to advertise: I have seen sexually explicit ads printed on the wrappers of condoms; ads printed on the backs of public bathroom stall doors; I've even seen an ad for a proctologist printed on the inside of a public toilet bowl—however, that was meant to be a joke. I recently read about a topless bar where the dancers had ads for various liquors temporarily tattooed on their buttocks.

Signs can even be used to make fun of a competitor; for instance, a plumber had rolls of toilet paper printed with the name of his most aggressive competitor printed on each panel of the paper. Such activities, however, may the run the risk of backfiring, inviting law suits and other forms of retaliation.

QUICK TIPS FOR SUCCESS

Signs offer cheap and effective advertising, if they are clever and are placed where people will respond to them. Signs can also be quite expensive; for example, I recently inquired about placing a thirty-foot sign at the entrance to the Midtown Tunnel, leading into Manhattan: The cost for an annual lease was $15,000 a month!

You can find many opportunities for effective signage that is far less expensive. Your signs should not only be unique and effective, but the placement of your signs should also be effective and, perhaps, unique. Look for new and unusual places to advertise the positive qualities of your products/services. I have seen ads printed on public benches, on baseball caps, on the sides of garbage trucks, on trash cans, on sidewalks; signs written in snow on sidewalks, in the dirt on cars, in lipstick on public mirrors—virtually everywhere. Indeed, wherever you look, you can find signs. Skywriters are even competing with the sun and clouds.

CHAPTER 8

LOW-COST PROMOTIONS THAT WORK

Whether I was carrying out marketing programs for my own various businesses or for those of my clients, I have always kept spending to a minimum. My businesses were born of ideas, not capital. Similarly, my clients have always been creative and diligent, but with limited funds for marketing and promoting their businesses. While they have understood that some money must be spent to achieve their marketing goals, they have not had the kinds of funds that major marketing and public relations agencies charge—that is, from $3,000 to $10,000 a month!

Every year, there are hundreds of thousands of people who open their own businesses. Many of them are laid-off managers and professionals, people who cannot find jobs that challenge them and pay them what they need. They cannot go to their local commercial banks and put up ideas for collateral. They cannot find partners who will finance their enterprises. And even loving relatives may be unwilling to turn over their hard-earned savings to dreamers whose dreams may not become mercantile realities.

In order to start a business, one must often become one's own patron. Successful self-patronage can turn an underfinanced business into one that generates handsome returns. Part of that self-patronage involves learning to market one's business cost-effectively. This chapter, by example and prescription, will help you execute the marketing ideas of this book as inexpensively as possible. Many of the following examples, with a few modifications, can be used to promote your business.

A BROADWAY-STYLE PREMIER FOR AN OUT-OF-TOWN DINER

About ten years ago, I helped a friend open a diner sixty-five miles outside of New York. There were numerous other diners within a five-mile radius of my friend. He had chosen the location because it was cheap, and he could not afford anything more expensive.

His opening was not exactly a Hollywood premier, but I decided to mimic one—after all, he needed something that would call attention to his diner and set it apart from all those others. To begin, I created flyers that announced, "Come and Meet the Stars of Big and Little Screens!" It gave a date, time, and address.

Next, I arranged to buy half-price tickets from a local movie theater; the tickets were for showings on Tuesday and Wednesday nights, when the theater had many empty seats. I gave the twenty tickets I had purchased to a local FM radio station. The station was attempting to increase the number of its listeners, and giving away tickets was a good way to create an incentive. The tickets would be awarded by the radio station to the first twenty people who showed up for our gala night of the stars. In addition, it ran a name-that-tune contest, offering winners free record albums.

On the night of the opening, the station agreed to broadcast directly from the diner. It even had a disc jockey who did an imitation of an old-style Hollywood gossip columnist; indeed, he would treat the event as if it were being attended by stars of the 1940s (he even sounded a bit like Walter Winchell). He would report on an apple-pie-eating contest, and a raffle for ten free three-course dinners.

To further simulate the luster of an old-fashioned Hollywood opening, I hired a large searchlight, which would rake the heavens as if looking for the unseeable.

Finally, I contacted a theatrical agency in New York City that represented numerous celebrity look-alikes. I hired about ten people who bore striking resemblances to the movie stars Barbara Streisand, Katharine Hepburn, Burt Reynolds, Paul Newman, James Dean, Marilyn Monroe, Humphrey Bogart, Sylvester Stallone, and Liza Minelli.

I called a local television news program and explained that we were putting on a parody of a Hollywood opening. Not only did I tell the producer who the look-alikes would be, I also told him that we would have a talent contest during which anyone who felt sufficiently inspired and talented would be invited to perform an imitation of any well-known entertainer. We had a carpenter friend build a small stage, six feet square, in front of the diner.

Three weeks prior to our spectacular Hollywood opening, I sent press releases and media alerts to the local daily and weekly newspapers.

More than three hundred people showed up to see the celebrity look-alikes; about a dozen people got up on the stage and sang and told jokes. As people arrived for the festivities, my friend operated a stand in the parking lot, selling hot dogs, pretzels, soda, and ice-cream cups. With each sale, he gave away a series of ten coupons that entitled the bearer to 15% off ten different meals at the diner. During all of this, our gigantic Cyclops of a searchlight roamed the sky.

Three local newspapers sent reporters and photographers. The radio had a remote set-up that permitted it to broadcast from the diner's parking lot; its reporter covered the event as if it were a genuine Hollywood opening. The television news program sent a cameraman, so the event was reported on the local evening news. Each of the celebrity look-alikes signed autographs with their real names.

Altogether, the event was a great success, and my friend built up a loyal following for his diner. Indeed, he was so successful that he sold the diner three years later and became a producer of industrial trade shows.

Because that event occurred more than a decade ago, I can no longer recall the exact costs. Prior to going ahead with such a promotion, you should make a list of all the elements, then call *at least five* vendors for each element. If some services or products are more than you can afford, ask vendors if there are less expensive options available.

Once you have assembled all the numbers, add them up. Can you afford the total cost? Will it generate sufficient business? Do you believe that your investment will deliver a profitable return? If you answer "yes" to all three questions, then proceed exuberantly but cautiously.

If you answer "no" to any of the questions, try to find a cheaper way of undertaking a similar promotion, one that will generate successful marketing results.

CHEAPER BY THE DOZEN

There are many other scaled-down events that one can undertake at a fraction of the cost of the "real thing."

One of my clients (who had very little money) decided that he would like to award customers of his urban pet shop a free romp in the woods with their dogs. He held a raffle, offering 12 people not only a free trip to the country for their dogs, but a gourmet outdoor meal served by a French chef.

Not wanting to than hide anything from the potential winners, he printed up posters that read: "Win a free afternoon in Van Cortlandt

Park in the picturesque Bronx. Have a picnic lunch served by a French chef. Free food for your dog, too!" He placed signs within a ten-block radius of his store, and handed out flyers inside the store.

When the winners were announced, he arranged for a school van to transport them and their canine pals to Van Cortlandt Park. Traveling with the happy pet owners was a recent graduate of a cooking school; he just happened to be from France.

Once they arrived in the park, the chef served them cold smoked salmon, asparagus, and truffles; Perrier water, and croissants. For dessert, they had fresh sliced melon and cheese. The dogs, of course, were given the very finest scraps, followed by an assortment of dog treats. Later in the afternoon, they all returned to the city. It proved to be such a successful and popular event that he repeated it every spring for seven years, until he retired and moved to Florida.

Success, of course, was measured by the dramatic boost in customers after each year's picnic. Pet owners seemed to love him, and not only patronized his store, but recommended it to others. As with the diner owner, he prepared a detailed "menu" of costs prior to the promotion. He cut out certain items, and made cheaper substitutions for ones that he thought too costly.

ACROSS THE LAKE AND INTO THE PARK

Another client awarded ten couples a cruise; he could not afford to send them to Europe or the Caribbean, so he gave them a cruise around the lake in Central Park. He hired ten rowboats and ten young men to row them; each of the young men wore a blue beret, a red-and-white striped shirt, white pants, and a red handkerchief tied around his neck. All of the couples who won cruises in the park had a delightful summer afternoon.

The promotion was on behalf of my client's restaurant; the couples who won boat rides had eaten at his restaurant. The men in the colorful rowing costumes were his waiters and busboys. The event was held early in the morning before the restaurant opened.

While the event generated only modest local news coverage, it did generate a considerable amount of good will for the restaurant. The owner took many photographs of the event, and placed them all over the restaurant. The photos of so many people having such a good time inspired other customers to participate in later events. At a very modest cost, he had created a pleasant and effective incentive for his customers.

YOU OUGHT TO BE IN PICTURES

While not everyone wants to cruise the lake in Central Park, most people would like to be in the movies. Very few, however, will experience the thrill of acting before a camera. If children are attending an after-school program that gives classes in dancing, acting, singing, and other performing arts, just imagine how excited they and their parents would be if each child got to perform in a movie.

One of my clients operated an after-school performing arts program; he received no government subsidies and relied solely on the tuition that parents paid for their children to attend. He himself was a film school graduate, and had acquired a variety of cinematic techniques and skills; he also owned video cameras, lights, and other equipment.

He prepared a direct mail piece with a photo of Shirley Temple on the cover. He wrote to parents of current students, as well as parents of students from past classes. Furthermore, he was able to buy a mailing list of parents who lived nearby, but whose children were not enrolled in his program. That list cost him $65 per 1,000 names; he had bought a list of about 3,000 names. He further reduced his costs by getting a bulk mail permit.

His letter to parents stated that children attending his program would be featured in a children's production of *Guys and Dolls*.

The production would be videotaped, and each parent would have the opportunity to purchase a copy of the tape for a modest sum. His offer had the desired effect, and his enrollment increased dramatically. Parents galore signed up their kids! At the end of the semester, parents bought videotapes of their kids performing in *Guys and Dolls*—and not just for themselves, but for grandparents and other relatives. Each tape, of course, was packaged in a case with the name of the after-school program, and the credits at the beginning and end gave my client additional unforgettable credit. Naturally, he included his address and phone number, too.

His costs were minimal, because he was able to do most of the work himself. He already owned the necessary equipment, and he was self-sufficiently skillful at using it.

AN ARTIST IN NEED

How about a portrait artist who can afford neither video equipment nor direct mail? Indeed, what if they can barely make a living? What is such a person to do?

Here's what one young aspiring artist did.

When I was in college, I attended an outdoor art show in Greenwich Village, where I saw some canvases that attracted my interest. I began speaking with the odd-looking young man who had painted them, and wound up purchasing one of his paintings for $25. He was intensely grateful and almost seemed to venerate me for having made a purchase.

Over the course of the next few months, I learned quite a lot about him. He lived in a one-room basement apartment in the East Village, between Avenues A and B. If parts of the East Village are dreary now, it was even more so in the 1960s. He had found much of his furniture on the streets, and had purchased a few additional necessities at the Salvation Army. When I visited his apartment, it was not just dreary, but dark and depressing. It had the faint commingling smells of vinegar, bleach, pipe tobacco, and cats. I visited there once, out of curiosity, and never returned.

I also learned that he had been raised by lower-middle-class parents in western Suffolk County on Long Island. He came from a large family; his siblings had either gotten civil service jobs or were manual laborers. He told me that he suffered from paranoid schizophrenia—at least, that's what a psychiatrist at some state mental institution had told him. As a result of unpredictable mood swings, which spanned from complete and almost catatonic withdrawals to red-faced bursts of rage, his parents had told him to leave their house.

Along the way, he had learned to paint—had taken lessons—and obviously had found some peace of mind in putting paint to canvas. To my amateur's eyes, he seemed better than merely competent, and his paintings had an obviously emotional quality that elicited the sympathy of viewers.

Added to his psychological problems was a physical limitation: when he was a young boy, he had fallen off his bicycle and broken his neck. As a result, he could not move his head and neck freely. Indeed, there were certain angles that his head and neck could not turn to. He walked around like one who has, not just a severe stiff neck, but excruciating muscle spasms–so that his eyes glared at you with the kind of intensity one sees in certain inspired maniacs. Though his gaze could certainly be frightening, he never lost his temper in my presence. He also managed to hold down a job as a dishwasher in some greasy spoon on Avenue C.

In addition to all of his more-or-less permanent indignities and sorrows, he suffered several more. In a period of ten months, his apartment was robbed three times. Each time, burglars carried away his radio, record player, hot plate, and electric clock.

One summer evening, he had either lost his keys or left them inside of his apartment. He did not have the keys to his apartment, and he did not have the key to the front door. He looked for the superintendent of the building, but could not find him, which was not unusual (the super was usually off drunk someplace when his tenants most required his services).

With no other option, my friend decided to climb through an unbarred window at the back of the shabby apartment building. A neighbor spotted him and called the police. Usually slow to arrive, that night the police responded in a matter of minutes. Shortly after he had managed to pick the lock to his own apartment, the police, with guns drawn, barged in like gangbusters and arrested him. After much questioning, they finally let him show some identification, and then released him.

That event, on top of everything else, caused my friend to descend into a dark pit of depression where he ruminated on his miserable existence for almost a week.

I decided to try to help him. Since it was unlikely that any art gallery would exhibit his work, I decided to create a one-man show for him, where he would sell all of his paintings.

These were, as I've written, unusual and interesting. He painted dark and forbidding landscapes; the tortured and/or troubled faces of dark young men; and the happy, seductive countenances of pale young women. His colors seemed in perfect harmony with the emotional quality of the paintings, and his brushstrokes seemed to contain all of his intense emotions.

I had another friend at that time who invested in real estate. He would buy and then renovate dilapidated brownstones. Once refurbished, the buildings would be put on the market and quickly sold for handsome profits. There were many people making a lot of money that way in the 1960s; in the 1970s, many of them turned to co-op conversions, where they made even more money, until the market finally collapsed in the late 1980s.

My real-estate friend had recently purchased an old brownstone on the Upper West Side. It had been used as a rooming house for more than twenty years, and when the owner died, her estate was eager to sell it. The interior had already been gutted, and I convinced my friend to let me use the ground floor as an art gallery for one week. If, however, things went as well as I thought they might, we would only need the gallery for a few days.

I took the young artist's paintings, about twenty altogether, and hung them throughout the space, which I had fully illuminated with

142

temporary lights. That Friday afternoon, at my suggestion, the artist began drawing faces on the sidewalk leading from the local IRT subway station. He drew rapidly, working with oil-based chalks, and concentrated intensely on his work. Each face covered several feet, and out of each mouth came a balloon containing words that implored people not to miss the chance of a lifetime. Other words urged pedestrians to see the leading new underground artist. ("Underground" was an important vogue word at the time; in fact, a popular magazine of the day had plastered signs throughout subway stations urging passersby to "Join The Underground. Read Evergreen Review.")

Other words on the sidewalk announced the arrival of a new young genius. "Genius," by the way, must be one of the most overused words in our lexicon. There are so many geniuses nowadays that there must be very few average people left in existence!

Along with words and faces, there were colorful drawings of arrows, spears, bullets, and rockets, all leading in the direction of the "gallery."

As home-bound commuters emerged from the subway station, they were greeted by two lovely young women dressed in leotards and tights; each wore a wreath of olive leaves in her hair, and one periodically played a flute. (They were aspiring actresses whom I knew at the time.) They danced around the surprised commuters, handing each one a flyer about the most exciting art event of the century. In fact, one of the young women got so carried away that she announced that those who visited our makeshift gallery were about to participate in a history-making event, one that would reverberate through the art history books as had the 1913 Armory Show, the first exhibition of Post-Impressionist Art, the arrival of the Dadaists in Paris, and even the exhibition of Picasso's *Guernica*! If for no other reason than simple curiosity, people took detours from their routes home, and visited the exhibition.

At the entrance to the ground-floor gallery stood a Jayne Mansfield look-alike in a silver lamé gown that flowed to the floor. The back of the dress was cut low to just below her waistline, and the front had a plunging neckline. She handed each visitor a list of paintings and a price list. The prices were modest, ranging from $275 to $450.

Inside, another actor, the father of one of my classmates, walked from painting to painting. He had a swept-back mane of elegant white hair and a neatly trimmed white goatee. He wore an old pin-striped blue suit and carried a gold-topped malacca cane. In one lapel of his blue suit, he sported a red rose. He carried a pad and pencil and was accompanied by his daughter, who pretended to be his secretary. In a booming voice, loud enough for everyone in the gallery to hear, he made certain comments calculated to sell paintings: "This fellow is, obviously, a genius. His mixes colors that other artists have never imagined. His brush strokes reveal a passionate intensity. I predict that in ten years, this young man's work will be in every major gallery. The Times should definitely do a story about this fellow; he's a real find. I'll have to speak to my editor on Monday. Once he becomes known, his prices will go through the roof."

Meanwhile, the artist humbly sat on a stool in the corner, where his mood was either one of curiosity or grimness. No one knew who he was. One eager patron asked him if there was a bathroom—the artist merely shrugged and looked as blank as a distant face in a photograph. The performance went on for three days, ending on Sunday evening after the last painting had been sold.

Altogether, we raised a little more than $7,000 for him, and we had all been volunteers. The more-than-grateful artist was able to leave his dingy hole-in-the-wall apartment. He moved to San Francisco, joining the flower children of that era. He had learned, like the character in *Being There*, that people will read the most astounding messages into a person's silences.

I eventually lost touch with him, but I hope he is happier today than when he lived in New York. He had, at least, one happy memory to take with him: the good will of people who were able to help free him from the shackles of an unhappiness he had been unable to break by himself.

AN AMERICAN DREAM: THE BEST EGG CREAM

A friend once introduced me to a young Russian immigrant. She had always wanted to come to America, but the Russian government had for years refused to let her leave. She spent her unhappy Russian confinement reading books about America, especially about New York City. Such books, I think, were not easy to obtain; whenever she got her hands on one, she pored over it as if it were a rare religious text with secret answers about the meaning of life. Her mind had become a scrapbook of imagined New York scenes, from the mid 1800s to the late 1960s. She not only wanted to come to New York, she wanted to open a business that she regarded as quintessentially New York.

What did she have in mind? An old-fashioned ice-cream parlor that served the best egg creams in the city. In addition, it would sell long pretzels, hamburgers on buns, cherry cokes, and French fries.

When the Russian government finally let her leave, via Italy, she got to New York and found a job in a jewelry store on West 47th Street in Manhattan. Though this street is the diamond capital of America, she was not happy there. She worked long hours and saved her money for more than three years. On weekends, she went to diners, coffee shops, and ice-cream parlors. She ordered her favorite dishes and asked how the cooks and waiters prepared everything. Her questions were extensive, and she required detailed answers. She not only wrote down all of the ingredients in a small reporter's notebook, but she also wrote down her evaluations of everything she ordered and ate. Items were rated with stars and numbers. She also wrote down, for example, how much chocolate syrup, seltzer, and milk were used in the most delicious egg creams.

In her small apartment in Queens, she experimented, recreating those items that had most caught her fancy. She worked diligently to improve each one, slightly changing the proportions of the ingredients.

She lived almost too frugally, saving all the money that would be needed to open her New York–style ice-cream parlor. One weekend, she was invited to a cousin's house in Brooklyn for dinner. She had few relatives and not many friends, so she eagerly accepted the invitation.

Her cousin had invited a young man who worked in the wholesale food business. The two got to talking about their shared interests; pretty soon, she was purring about her dreams and ambitions. He was noticeably charmed and asked her out.

Six months later, they were married in a civil ceremony at City Hall. They moved into a two-bedroom apartment in Queens, and used one bedroom as an office.

As a loving husband, wanting to help his new wife succeed, he found a store for her, put up much of the necessary capital, and helped her open the store of her dreams.

Though it was outfitted like an old-fashioned ice-cream parlor, it could not have been in a worse location. There was no school nearby, so teenagers would not be dropping in after school. In addition, the only nearby businesses relied little on off-the-street customers: there was an insurance office, a lawyer's office, a real estate agency, a small print shop, and a dentist's office. In other words, the block was not under attack by hordes of aggressive retail shoppers!

To attract people to the store, I decided to do tie-ins with merchants who were no more than ten blocks away. As a result, I was able to get a movie theater to hand out discount coupons to all ticket purchasers. Similarly, I arranged for a supermarket, a dry cleaning store, and a card shop to hand out discount coupons. They all agreed to the promotion because we offered them one free meal every day. It was worth it to us, for business dramatically increased.

146

I needed something special, however; something that would create an aura and a name recognition which would continue to generate business.

First, I decided to create an international egg-cream-tasting contest. I invited reporters from local weekly papers to sample and rate a dozen varieties of egg creams, and I also invited all amateur egg-cream aficionados to sample the same. If an amateur aficionado chose as best the same egg cream as the experts, that person would win one free egg cream every week for five years.

The event was accompanied by music from an enormous 1950s Wurlitzer jukebox. The husband had a business acquaintance who leased the jukebox to us for a nominal sum. Egg-cream sippers got to hear songs that were hits in 1945, in 1960, and all the years in between. The store's four employees dressed as 1950s teenagers: jeans with rolled cuffs and white T-shirts for the two boys, who had swept-back and greased pompadours, and long sideburns. The two girls had their hair pulled back into ponytails, and wore white blouses with circle pins at the neck, pleated red plaid skirts, white socks, and saddle shoes. The owner of the store had paid for the outfits, which cost less than $400.

Large posters of Elvis, James Dean, and Marilyn Monroe hung on one wall. We even rented a super-chromed Harley Davidson for the day from one of the owner's friends and parked it near the cash register.

As a result of sending out press releases and media alerts, the store not only got publicity from local weekly newspapers, but one of the local television news programs covered the event as well. The following day, a disc jockey from a station that played the hit songs of 1950s and 60s spoke about the event, and urged his listeners to try our delicious egg creams.

To keep the momentum going, and to add to the success, I arranged with a retailer of above-ground pools to create the largest egg cream in New York history. The retailer donated the use of an above-ground swimming pool because he anticipated business-generating publicity. Into the large plastic pool, about 15 feet in diameter and 3 feet deep, we poured about 18 inches in depth of cool, delicious egg cream. Hundreds of extra-long straws were given away to people who wanted to drink directly from the pool; others were given glasses for dipping.

Such events are always worth a certain amount of news coverage, and this was no exception. Television, radio, and newspapers all turned out to cover New York's first and, as far we knew, only egg cream in a swimming pool. The pool retailer was happy, for the publicity spoke about his pools as well as the egg cream. Both businesses benefited from the event, and it cost them very little. My client had merely to buy the ingredients for an enormous egg cream and the pool retailer had to pay someone to clean his swimming pool.

QUICK TIPS FOR SUCCESS

I'm sure that there are numerous inexpensive promotions that you can create for your business, too. If you are having difficulty thinking of something, read newspapers and magazines, and watch television news programs.

You may also want to look through the *Guinness Book of Records* for ideas, as well as through old issues of *Life* magazine.

There are also magazines that report on inventive and successful promotions; following are the names, addresses, and telephone numbers of several of the best.

1. *Creative, The Magazine of Promotion & Marketing* (212) 840-0160
   37 West 39 Street
   New York, NY 10018
2. *Public Relations Journal* (212) 460-1413
   33 Irving Place
   New York, NY 10003
3. *Adweek* (212) 536-5336
   1515 Broadway
   New York, NY 10036
4. *The Ragan Report* (312) 335-4377
   212 W. Superior St. #200
   Chicago, IL 60610
5. *Marketing Management* (312) 831-2794
   250 S. Wacker Drive #200
   Chicago, IL 60606

CHAPTER 9

Win–Win Promotions: Contests, Raffles, and Coupons

Most people would love to get something for nothing, or for very little—this is the underlying motive for all gambling. Las Vegas is not heaven for people who believe that money is the reward of hard work. The millions of people who buy state lotto tickets do not imagine they will make tens of millions of dollars by being another Henry Ford or Bill Gates. At some point, virtually everyone has dreamt of having enormous wealth—and getting it for nothing.

While working is the time-honored way of achieving wealth, there are many people who know that they will spend their lives living from paycheck to paycheck. One compensation is to dream, regardless of how unlikely it may be, of being presented with some sort of windfall. Just look at states that offer tens of millions of dollars to lucky lotto winners. In each of those states, there are hundreds of thousands (if not millions) of people lined up to take a chance. Increase the amount of the prize, and one increases the number of those who will buy a ticket to the land of their dreams.

Marketers know this, too.

It is why companies offer rebates, discount coupons, prizes, and sweepstakes. These have proven, time and time again, that if consumers are offered something for buying a product, they will—indeed—buy the product.

On a smaller scale than General Mills or Kellogg, you too can provide your customers with something in exchange for buying your products.

RAFFLES, SWEEPSTAKES, AND COUPONS

A number of years ago, I had a client who created raffles, sweepstakes, and other contests as a means of increasing sales for his clients. My job was to promote my client's expertise to companies that wanted an effective and proven means of dramatically increasing their sales and profits.

Before I continue, you should understand that while raffles may cost money, one cannot require a consumer to purchase a product in order to participate in a sweepstakes. Anyone, whether customer or not, has a legal right to enter a sweepstakes without making a purchase. Coupons, an entirely different species of animal, can be given away, or be included in a product that one buys.

My client would put together marketing programs that included sweepstakes, raffles, and/or coupons, each working as an incentive that would increase sales. While he worked on behalf of very large companies, many of the techniques that he employed can also be used for smaller businesses, such as yours.

COUPONS

The simplest kind of promotion that we would do is something you have probably participated in countless times: clipping a coupon from the back of a cereal box, mailing it to a redemption center with a cash-register receipt as proof of purchase, and receiving a token gift. Kids are always mailing away for secret rings, laser guns, magic talismans, sports memorabilia, dolls, celebrity photos, and other items. While parents probably do not care about such trivia, their children urge them to buy certain cereals just so they can get whatever the company is offering that week or month. (I recall that when I was about six years old, I bought a square inch of the North Pole for a dollar.)

PRIZES

One of the classic incentives for kids was buying a box of Cracker Jacks, and getting a free prize at the bottom of the box. You always had to get to the bottom of the box to get the prize, which meant that you either ate the contents or poured it out. That, in turn, meant that you were ready to buy another box to get another prize. All of this went on every week, insuring the folks who made Cracker Jacks that they would not only have new customers, but that new customers would become repeat customers as well. And they got all those customers for the price of plastic whistles, plastic rings, and other cheap toys that were invariably lost and forgotten. It didn't matter; kids couldn't wait till their parents took them to the supermarket for yet another box of Cracker Jacks!

MONEY-BACK REBATES

For one client, we created a $5 rebate. In other words, if you bought our product, clipped a coupon from the package, and sent it to a redemption center with a proof of purchase, you would receive by return mail a check for $5. It was hardly different from the idea of sending in a box top and getting a Buck Rogers Magic Ray Gun. The client not only succeeded in getting retailers to buy his products because of the rebate promotion, but the rebate, which was heavily advertised, resulted in rapid turns (which is marketing terminology for accelerated sales).

THE HIGH COST OF INCENTIVES

When companies run successful promotions, they invariably spend a lot of money on advertising. For example, coupons and/or rebate offers are regularly advertised in the Sunday supplements of newspapers, special free-standing inserts (FSIs), and in-store circulars.

For example, I once helped to introduce a new frozen food product. We arranged to advertise the product with a cents-off coupon in Sunday color supplements, FSIs, and in-store circulars. Each coupon entitled a purchaser to a 50-cent reduction on the cost of the item.

Sales incentives obviously encourage people to purchase products, especially if the incentive is a free product or one that is sold at a steep discount.

THE ANSWER FOR THE SMALL BUSINESS

Unfortunately, most small companies, unless very lucky and unusually creative, are unable to offer the kind of promotions that are regularly part of a large company's marketing agenda. There are ways, however, of bartering time and services so that you can create the kinds of promotions that will have a dramatic impact on sales.

Here is an example of something I was able to do for a small over-the-counter pharmaceutical company. I wrote a how-to health-care article that was published in several magazines. It featured a number of my client's products. At the end of the article, readers were invited to purchase any two of my client's products, send in box tops from the products with the cash register receipt(s), and receive a check for $1.00. The promotion worked very well and was relatively inexpensive, so we decided to expand it. I rewrote the article and had it made into a two-color brochure. Instead of offering a rebate, we offered a coupon that could be clipped or torn from the brochure. Customers were instructed to present it to a cashier at the time of purchase of any two of my client's products, and they would receive a $1.00 discount.

153

The brochure was given to thousands of independent drugstores as well as to major drugstore chains. They all placed it at the cash-register counters, so that it became an effective P-O-P incentive.

It offered not only valuable and helpful health information that would benefit consumers, but an attractive discount as well. In addition, many drugstores have regular charge-account customers, and we made arrangements for many of those stores to include our brochure in their monthly mailing of invoices. It was good for the stores, because their customers perceived it as a valuable piece of information being distributed as a public service. Sales increased significantly, not just for the products we offered at that time, but for other products that became available in the near future. We had built customer loyalty by showing that we cared.

PREMIUM INCENTIVES

In addition to participating in promotions, you can also increase your sales by selling your products as premium incentives.

What is a premium incentive?

The answer is best given by an example. As I noted briefly in the Introduction, I once had a student who designed and manufactured presentation cases for photographers, and I suggested that he go to a photo trade show at the Javits Center in New York. This is an annual event, during which many manufacturers exhibit their wares while customers roam the aisles looking for appropriate bargains. The customers are typically large corporations that want to buy inexpensive products, which they can then make available to their own customers as incentives for doing business.

My student, being a smaller-than-small manufacturer, could hardly afford to rent a booth at the show. He merely walked the aisles, carrying his cases, some under his arms, others in his hands, and showing them to possible customers. After about two hours, he had sold $300,000 worth of cases to two European camera manufacturers! They would use his cases as premium incentives. In other words, every time a prospective customer showed interest in purchasing several thousand dollars worth of camera equipment, that customer was told about the free, elegant leather case that the camera company was offering. The case was a premium incentive that encouraged a customer to buy camera equipment from one manufacturer rather than another.

I strongly recommend that anyone who manufactures consumer products attend the Premium Incentive Show. If you cannot, then be sure to subscribe to Incentive Magazine, 355 Park Avenue South, New York, NY 10010, (212) 592-6453. It will give you a wealth of valuable ideas.

Through the years, I have helped many clients sell products to large companies, rather than to individual consumers. Their products were subsequently awarded as premium incentives or, in some cases, sold at steep discounts. It hardly mattered to my clients, for they made large bulk sales without having to sell products to thousands of individual customers. Not only was the bookkeeping simple, but so were the bank deposit slips.

BIKES FOR TYKES

Here's another example of a successful sale of merchandise as a premium incentive. Several years ago, a distributor of bicycles came to me because he was suffering from slumping sales. I suggested we hire a salesperson, someone expert in making premium-incentive sales. Rather than paying that person a salary, we were able to hire him on a commission basis. After only two months, he succeeded in making a highly remunerative sale to a large cereal company. His commission on that sale was larger than a salary would have been, and my client received a substantial windfall.

Many children across America may now be riding my client's bikes, which they got at attractively reduced prices. It was one of those promotions where everybody won.

155

I have also helped to sell pens, exercise equipment, toys, vitamins, videotapes, video games, and books, among other products, as premium incentives. In all cases, my clients were able to reap large rewards that would have been out of their reach if they had tried to sell directly to consumers.

OBTAINING PRIZES

If premium incentive sales are not possible for your business (because you are a retailer, or have a service business), you may want to put together a promotion that requires the awarding of prizes. In that case, you must find a way of getting prizes without paying for them.

Obtaining prizes for clients' promotions is something that I have done many times over the years. I have had to come up with incentives, so that other manufacturers would be willing to donate their merchandise to my clients. Why would a manufacturer donate anything at all? If, let's say, you donated 25 dolls, would you accept as payment a wealth of free advertising for your products on radio and television, and in magazines?

Of course, you would!

It would be well worth it. In fact, some manufacturers are so eager to be included in contest promotions that they will ask when the next promotion will take place, so they can provide additional merchandise!

YOUR PRODUCTS AS AWARDS

This approach is similar to having your products awarded as prizes on television quiz shows. The products featured on those shows are not there because the producer fell in love with them and wanted to award them to lucky contestants. Rather, the production companies of television quiz shows receive what's euphemistically called "a consideration" for featuring certain products as prizes on the shows.

At the conclusion of such a program, photos of the prizes are often shown again, the name of the manufacturer is stated, and often an announcer adds that a "consideration" has been paid by the manufacturer.

In addition to quiz shows, there are television sit-coms and dramas, as well as movies. Many people may be unaware that when they see products in a kitchen or on a supermarket shelf in a movie, the manufacturer has paid a hefty fee for that exposure.

I once arranged, for example, to have a food product in an action comedy. At a certain moment, the leading character opens a kitchen cabinet in his girlfriend's apartment, and there are rows and rows of my client's products. Voila! That nonspeaking role for the products cost my client $35,000!

WHAT NOT TO DO

Unfortunately, many unsophisticated merchants have told me that they have sent dozens of free samples of their products to television newscasters and talk-show hosts. They had hoped that their products would be warmly received and get an on-air plug. "Don't bother," I would tell each of them. Such free advertising is highly unlikely. It may happen once in a very great while, but not enough to effect an increase in sales and profits. Nevertheless, many thousands of optimists send their products to television and radio personalities, hoping for, if not expecting, free endorsements. It rarely happens. They usually get back a letter that has gone out hundreds, if not thousands of times, thanking the donor for his or her kindness. (After all, television personalities do not want to offend even one potential member of the audience that can contribute to their ratings.)

WHAT TO DO

Instead of sending free samples of one's products to celebrities, one should work creatively to set up promotions that will get results. If it means you have to get prizes, then bring in a local radio station or weekly newspaper as your partner—they will likely want to increase their listenership or readership. If you manufacture or are an exclusive distributor of a product, you can use that product to barter for free advertising that may be worth hundreds of thousands of dollars.

PENS ON TV

Here's an example that was worth many thousands of dollars to a client. In 1976, I worked for one of the largest public relations companies in the world. One of the many clients I helped was a company called Pilot Pens; though I was not their account manager, I was asked to provide some help.

I knew a producer at "Wonderama," an extremely popular children's television show during the 1970s. I arranged to create a palette of Pilot Pens in every available color. Each week, the show would have a contest and would award one child in the audience a complete selection of pens.

Pilot Pens were not only displayed on the palette before and after each contest, but the name was mentioned repeatedly on the air. Hundreds of thousands of little kids got to know about the wonderful virtues of Pilot Pens, and it cost the pen company only a weekly supply of pens! Of course, the company also had to pay us a monthly retainer, but it was a small price for such regular and prominent advertising.

BOOKS, EXERCISE, AND TV

Here's another example of a contest that worked wonders for a publisher and a book store. A number of years ago, as the coauthor of a book on physical fitness, I was traveling the country on a book-promotion tour. My coauthor and I traveled to about fifteen cities; in each, we did at least one radio, one television, and one newspaper interview. Some cities offered additional opportunities.

In one case, we arranged to put on an exercise class in a book-store. On a local morning television show, we announced that the first 20 people who came to the XYZ book store would not only receive a free exercise class, but they would also get the book at 50% off the cover price.

The book store had paid 50% of the cover price for the book, but it had 100 copies in stock. If they could get enough people in the store to sell all 100 copies, they would make a 50% profit on 80 copies, while 20 would be a wash.

In other words, they got nearly 10 minutes of free television advertising time by selling 20 books at the price they had paid for them! Thereafter, the store worked with other television and radio programs to do similar promotions.

It also turned out to be a terrifically effective marketing device for us, for we sold all 100 books! During the course of the television interview, we had also stated that we would provide personalized autographs on each copy of our book, and would answer all questions relating to fitness goals and give specific exercises to accomplish those goals.

BASEBALL INCENTIVES

For the manufacturer of the model baseball stadium described in Chapter 1, I created a contest that included a sales incentive as well. Each model was packaged with five vintage baseball cards. In three models, we placed one card worth from $5 to $20. Further-more, we placed a raffle ticket in each model, the cost of which was included in the purchase price. Customers only had to fill out their raffle tickets with name and address, then mail them to the man-ufacturer with a cash register receipt. We would pick one winner, and that person would receive a pair of tickets for box seats to two Yankees home games.

Each model was shrinkwrapped, and sported a large label in bold, bright red letters that announced the inclusion of the baseball cards and raffle tickets for two Yankees home games. It worked just as we had hoped, and several thousand people, all of whom were baseball fans, purchased the stadium model and entered the contest. The cost to my client was modest, but the results were greater than they had hoped.

AMERICA'S MOST BEAUTIFUL BABY

I had client who manufactured and distributed a series of over-the-counter pharmaceutical products for babies. I decided that, since my client did no consumer advertising, we needed a special promotion to generate consumer awareness.

I created a simple contest, called America's Most Beautiful Baby. In a press release announcing the contest, I wrote that the winning baby's face would be used on my client's packages and, perhaps, on in-store posters and point-of-purchase materials. All a mother had to do was send my client a photo of her baby, the baby's birth date, and one sentence describing her baby's appearance. Babies could be from 4 weeks to 18 months old. The winning baby also would receive a U.S. Savings Bond to be used for the child's education.

In addition, each parent was asked to include a self-addressed, stamped envelope. In that envelope, we placed a pamphlet dealing with common childhood maladies, a list of local drugstores that carried my client's products, and cents-off coupons for all of their baby products.

Numerous publications published my press release, resulting in many thousands of responses. Several months later, my client chose ten semifinalists. The photos of the ten babies were sent with another press release to newspapers and magazines. The publicity was enormous. Finally, my client chose the winning baby, and had a party for the baby and her parents in New York. At the party, the baby was presented to the media. A number of publications and television news programs ran stories about the Most Beautiful Baby in America.

Not only did my client get considerable amounts of publicity, both before and after the contest, but parents used the cents-off coupons to purchase products for their babies and became loyal customers.

IDEAS FOR WIN–WIN PROMOTIONS

While some promotions are easy to create, others are not. Many people have difficulty coming up with promotions that are suitable for their businesses. Indeed, many of my students are often frustrated, for they are unable to think of promotions that will benefit them. Good promotions, I often tell them, can come from a variety of sources. For example, one day, I was walking by a church, and someone asked me to buy a raffle ticket. The winner would win a brand new GEO Metro. I asked the woman who sold me the raffle ticket how the church had obtained the new Metro. She said that the local Chevrolet dealer was a member of the congregation, and he wanted to do something to help the church. He wrote off the gift as a charitable donation, and worked with the church to sell more than a 1,500 raffle tickets at $20 each. The church earned $30,000 for much-needed repairs, and the dealer got a tax write-off while doing something that would benefit others.

The people who had purchased raffle tickets probably did not miss the $20, for that, too, was a charitable donation. And, since the winner was a woman they all knew, they were happy that a friend or acquaintance had been the beneficiary.

While many churches—I'm sure—organize similar raffles, there are few, if any, for-profit businesses that also do. It gave me an idea.

I represented a quartet of classical musicians who traveled throughout New England putting on chamber music concerts. They were all highly talented and well-trained musicians; they obviously loved playing music and, as an ensemble, they were superb. They often got foundations to underwrite a part of their costs. There

161

were ever more candidates for foundation money, however, and my clients were unable to raise the kind of money they needed to underwrite many of their concerts.

Using the same principle as the church, I asked the musicians to supply me with a mailing list of contributors and their occupations. On their list were three car dealers who happened to love classical music. The musicians had long put on their concerts as part of a non-profit program; a portion of anyone's donation to them was tax deductible. I wrote to all three car dealers asking if they would be willing to sell us a car based upon our paying for it at a time in the future. In other words, we would raffle off the car, pay the dealer his invoiced cost from our proceeds, and keep the balance to cover the group's costs. I urged them to do this not only because of their love of chamber music, but also because of the free publicity that I was sure I could obtain for them. In addition, I offered them free lifetime tickets to every local concert that my clients put on.

One said no; the second wanted to think about it, which I suspected would also mean no; but the third dealer agreed almost spontaneously, and gave us a brand new Ford Taurus. We used a small army of friends and family to make telephone solicitations, and I created a direct-mail campaign as well. As with the church, we sold thousands of raffle tickets, and earned more money than we had from any individual concert. When the money was counted, we were able to pay the dealer for his invoiced cost of the car, and still have many thousands of dollars left for concerts!

REAL ESTATE FOR NEXT TO NOTHING

At the time when I owned a gymnastics and exercise school, I wanted to extend my market as cheaply as possible. I looked upon various suburban areas as potential markets, but I did not want to invest hundreds of thousands of dollars to open fitness facilities in each of those markets. In fact, even if I wanted to, I could not afford to do so.

Instead, I contacted Bloomingdale's department stores. I suggested to a vice-president at one of the stores that each store put on a make-over/shape-over clinic. In other words, women could come into each of several stores, take an exercise class, have their hair cut, and get a facial that included being made up by a professional make-up artist. Not only would Bloomingdale's attract many new customers, but they would have the opportunity to sell them generous supplies of expensive cosmetics. I further suggested that we offer exercise classes for babies and toddlers, since mothers would be unable to get haircuts and make-overs if they had to watch their children. Those children were, of course, too young to be in school, but not too young to be in our exercise classes.

Bloomingdale's not only advertised the program in daily newspapers, but also mailed announcements to its customers. The response was overwhelming, for more people wanted to participate than we could accommodate.

Even better: the clinics laid the groundwork for opening independent exercise programs for women and children in three suburban neighborhoods. Other than labor costs, Bloomingdale's had absorbed all of our other costs, particularly the cost of advertising, which was substantial.

WIN A PRIZE, BUY A HOUSE

Perhaps the most notorious form of "something for nothing" is the one generated by real-estate development companies. You may have received a letter in the mail announcing that you have won a free color television. In order to claim your prize, you must drive several hours to a real-estate development site, and listen to several additional hours of high-pressured salesmanship. At the end of your ordeal, you get to own a television set, which you may want to kick apart rather than watch.

The point of the sales pitch is to get you to buy a house, or to sign up for a time-share in a vacation village. The salespeople are so successful at converting potential customers into actual customers that they can afford to give away prizes. (After all, if they weren't successful, they would stop!)

Again, it's that old saw that everyone wants something for nothing. If you can give someone an inexpensive product as an inducement to buy an expensive one, then you have succeeded. The underlying nature of all incentives is to give something for nothing or for very little, so that people will be induced to pay for something else.

VIVA LAS VEGAS!

I began this chapter by discussing Las Vegas and gambling. Here is an example of the ultimate Vegas incentive. Years ago, I knew the man who invented the Las Vegas junket; it was a brilliant concept that resulted in countless millions of dollars for the casinos.

The visionary who started the junkets would get lists of "high rollers" from various casinos. He would invite each of them to fly to Vegas for a weekend, free of charge. In addition to giving them free air travel, he also arranged for them to stay (at no cost) in the most beautiful and luxurious VIP rooms in one of the casinos. In Las Vegas terminology, this is called "comping" the guest. In other words, the high rollers did not have to pay for anything other than their gambling. The casino paid all costs; in exchange, the high rollers gambled away hundreds of thousands of dollars.

The man who had organized the event got a commission based on how much money the high rollers lost.

Needless to say, he became a millionaire!

QUICK TIPS FOR SUCCESS

In this chapter, I have provided examples of how marketers appeal to a basic human desire to get something for nothing, or for well below cost.

As a means of doing so, marketers use coupons, raffles, sweepstakes, contests, premium incentives, and cross promotions. Such devices have proven extremely effective in helping manufacturers and retailers sell a wide variety of products.

There is also the opportunity to create win–win promotions between businesses. Such win–win promotions are often barter agreements of products/services for free adverting or publicity.

There are many and varied opportunities for you to market your products/services by using the techniques described in this chapter.

CHAPTER 10

The Envelope, Please: Awards That Promote Your Business

Awards can be wonderfully effective marketing tools. The Academy Awards, probably the most popular awards in the world, command the attention of a celebrity-hungry audience that will spend vast sums of money after viewing the recipients of Oscars. Indeed, the Academy Awards were created not merely to promote movies and the beautiful actors who are their twinkling stars, but as marketing tools as well. Obviously, a movie upon which special awards have been bestowed is going to draw in millions of independent minds—who will spend millions of dollars to enjoy a product that is deserving of esteem. In addition, any star who also receives an Academy Award will not only enjoy the acclaim of the movie-going public, but will become a more high-priced and marketable commodity than they had been prior to receiving an Oscar.

In fact, the Oscars are so valuable and effective that they often confirm public images that may be entirely misleading. There are, for example, macho tough guys who are actually anything but tough, and will go out of their way to avoid confrontations; there are also sexy femmes fatales whose sexual images may not correspond to reality. It doesn't matter to the public: the parts have been played; the awards have confirmed the images; the show must go on; and, of course, the money pours in.

MODEST AWARDS FOR SMALL BUSINESS

More modest awards can win honors for small businesses, or for some commendable professionals. In all cases, awards can serve to promote something or someone.

And small businesses can certainly learn from the flamboyant awards associated with show business. From Broadway, from the music industry, from television, and even from cable television, one can learn a great deal about how awards can be used as marketing tools. If properly publicized, awards are not only effective marketing tools, but can also generate a considerable amount of business.

An award is a recognition for excellence. That same message applies whether one is a movie star, a dog handler, a chef, or an honor student.

With rare exceptions, people love to receive awards. And if the recipient has an outsized ego, awards feed that ego and confirm one's high self-opinion.

I have long witnessed how effective awards can be as marketing tools, and I have often used awards to increase sales for my clients. Previous examples that I have given include the Heros of Young America Award given by *The World Almanac*, and the awarding of the stadium model to media figures (both in Chapter 1), and the award to a Brooklyn Congressman for his "support" of low-income housing (in Chapter 5, where I have devoted a section to testimonials and awards). What follows are additional examples that, I hope, will give you some ideas for promoting your own business.

THE MOST BEAUTIFUL HAND CONTEST

Having conducted a contest for years called "The Most Beautiful Feet in America," I decided to run a similar contest for another client. It, too, would conclude with an award that would boost sales. While the promotion of contests is a good way to publicize a business, the bestowing of an award on the winner provides an additional opportunity to gain valuable publicity.

"The Most Beautiful Hand Contest" was put on for a jewelry company called Shenoa. I began by creating a provocative press release, in which I noted that the winner would receive not only a diamond ring but a $100 U.S. Savings Bond; in addition, the winner's hand would appear in some of Shenoa's advertising of wedding and engagement rings.

New Woman magazine, one of the more popular monthly women's magazines, ran a story entitled "Give A Hand," shown in Exhibit 10-1. The response was greater than I had expected: hundreds of women sent in photos of their hands. The contest ran for three months, then a winner was chosen. A photo of her beauti-

EXHIBIT 10-1   Awards are a good way to promote someone or something. Here is a story *New Woman* magazine ran about "The Most Beautiful Hand Contest" which was sponsored by Shenoa, a company which received much attention as a result of their contest.

GIVE A HAND

Most of us have accepted the fact that we don't look like Cindy Crawford. But if you still crave a shot at modeldom, try this: Shenoa, an American designer and retailer of diamond rings, is sponsoring the "America's Most Beautiful Hand Contest." The winner will receive a diamond ring and a $100 U.S. Savings Bond and will be flown to New York City to have her hands photographed for the Shenoa spring advertising campaign. To enter, send a photo of your hands to Shenoa, 1 W. 47th St., New York, NY 10036. The contest ends February 1, 1996. Call (212) 764-1625 for more details.

From NEW WOMAN, December 1995, p.28. © NEW WOMAN, "Beauty Marks" column. Reprinted with permission.

ful hand and a press release were distributed to a wide variety of women's publications. Many of them ran our story and, in doing so, dramatically increased Shenoa's sales of wedding and diamond engagement rings.

AWARDS TO INANIMATE OBJECTS

One can even give awards to inanimate objects. Several years ago, for example, I hired two college students to survey approximately 500 New Yorkers about the most beautiful edifices in Manhattan, as well as the ugliest. The survey was commissioned by a commercial interior design company that I represented.

When the survey was completed, I wrote a press release entitled "The Ten Ugliest Sites; The Ten Most Beautiful Sites in NYC." It generated feature stories in tabloid newspapers, real estate publications, and construction publications, and comments on local television news programs. In every story, my client was mentioned as having commissioned the survey. In some cases, there was even a small amount of controversy over the choices. Some people added their own ugliest sites, while others had their candidates for the most beautiful. The result, of course, was that my client had been rendered an arbiter of good taste, which was appropriate for a business that deals in beautiful objects.

BEST DRESSED BABY

Babies invariably arouse feelings of affectionate amusement in most people. One year, I decided to hold an awards ceremony for the Best Dressed Baby, on behalf of a children's clothing store. Mothers and fathers showed up with babies in clothes that could have inspired Hollywood costume designers! There were babies in the usual cute and expensive snow suits, but there were also babies in sequined gowns and little fur coats—there was even one in a tiny tuxedo and top hat. The winner's parents were awarded $500 worth of free baby clothing. All the others received free mittens, and 20% discount coupons toward the purchase of baby clothing.

In order to get parents to participate in the contest and attend the selection of the winner, we had taken out small ads in neighborhood newspapers and sent out press releases. A photo of the winner, accompanied by a press release, was sent to weekly newspapers and baby magazines.

PUPPY AWARDS

Puppies seem to inspire many of the same feelings that babies do. With that in mind, I decided to hold an awards ceremony for the Best Dressed Pooch, on behalf of a pet shop. Again, I had taken out small ads in weekly newspapers while also sending out press releases announcing the contest. More than fifty dog owners showed up. Not only were dogs garbed in the usual fancy dog coats and jeweled collars, but some wore boots and stockings, some wore short pants, and others wore ruffles. One had on a bonnet, and another a pair of rubber antlers. The winner was chosen and a photo was taken, which was later sent with a press release to all the newspapers that had helped us publicize the contest. The winner got a 50 lb. bag of kibble and a case of canned dog food; all the contestants received 5 free dog biscuits. As in the previous contest, the participants also received discount coupons for the purchase of all pet supplies. The contest, the awards ceremony, and the subsequent publicity all caused a dramatic upsurge in business.

ENVIRONMENTAL HAZARDS

One can recognize negative, rather than postitive, attributes. For example, instead of the Best Dressed list, one could compile the Worst Dressed list. In keeping with that approach, I had a client who put together a list of the most environmentally hazardous sites in New York. Hers was a company that did environmental assess-ments for landlords, banks, insurance companies, and mortgage companies. At the time of our survey, the concept of "sick building syndrome" was very much in the news. (This term refers to those buildings that can make one sick because the air in the buildings is improperly filtered, and may contain a variety of pollutants that can cause varying degrees of illness.)

My client had actually gone around the city measuring the air quality of subway stations, public buildings, tunnels, air-conditioned buses, as well as apartment buildings that were built over roadways or near bridges. I wrote a press release entitled "Where It's Dangerous To Live And Work." We not only got many print and television news stories, but my client was interviewed by several reporters and appeared on *Geraldo*. Altogether, the result was that she was positioned as a leading expert on environmental issues facing tenants in commercial and residential buildings. That, in turn, led to a significant increase in her consulting business.

BUGGED

Here is yet another example that might inspire you. Years ago, I represented someone just starting out in the exterminating business. In order to get attention for him, we performed a survey in which we asked people, "What insects bug you the most?"

The responses included cockroaches, mosquitoes, ants, spiders, ticks, fleas, and bees. To publicize the results, rather than sending out a press release, we held a press conference called "The Most Hated Bugs." On a table, in jars, were samples of the "winners." Each jar received an award consisting of miniature fly swatters. The roaches, for example, were awarded five fly swatters, while the bees got only one. My client passed out to those in attendance a two-panel pamphlet about how to control pests. Following the press conference and the ensuing publicity, my client sent to all those whom we had surveyed reprints of articles that had publicized our Most Hated Bug Awards. In addition, he sent them 20%-off coupons to be used when they hired my client to rid their homes of pests.

QUICK TIPS FOR SUCCESS

Remember: the media loves unusual stories about pets and babies, so if you have a logical means of using either to promote your business, chances are that you will get the kind of publicity that will attract the attention of customers.

Think of awards that you can present in a dramatic, attention-grabbing way. You must also choose candidates who will be of interest to the media, either because they are celebrities, or because they have accomplished something newsworthy.

If what you do is successful, you can turn it into an annual event, one that will be worth many thousands of dollars in increased sales. Several of my clients have even trademarked their contests and awards because they regard their events as such valuable marketing tools.

CHAPTER 11

To Err Is Human; To Succeed Takes Patience: Mistakes To Avoid, Secrets To Keep In Mind

Even the greatest public relations and marketing professionals make mistakes. They may not admit it, for doing so can dent the glittering armor of one's professional reputation. For non-professionals, however, inexperience can be the mother of mistakes that you would like to disown. If you are aware of the most common mistakes, you will significantly reduce your chances of bringing them into the world.

This chapter tells how to handle five common mistakes that often undermine the potential success of an otherwise sound marketing and public relations program.

MISTAKE #1: MAKING BAD PUBLICITY WORSE

If you happen to get bad publicity, don't shine a spotlight on that publicity. Don't breathe additional life into bad news. The most common instances of this occur when a person who should know better has made a mistake that is publicly reported. Rather than admitting the mistake, putting it into a reasonable perspective, and going on to more important issues, people often either deny the mistake, or attempt to blame it on another person. Such self-serving behavior is often transparently false, and only serves to further diminish one's credibility and stature.

Since everyone makes mistakes, anyone who doesn't have a heart of stone can identify with your plight. If there are justifying reasons for having made a mistake, tell a reporter about those reasons. Don't hide behind a wall of false invulnerability. If you can engage a reporter's sympathy, chances are that the public will forgive you too.

ACCIDENTS HAPPEN

Here's an example of how an unfortunate accident can be used to demonstrate your good will and responsibility. When I owned a gymnastics school, one of my students fell off the uneven parallel bars and broke her leg. We rushed her to a nearby hospital, sat with her in the emergency room, and comforted her as her leg was being set and put in a cast. We had called her mother, who was at work at the time of the accident. She met us at the hospital and was grateful that we had brought her daughter to the emergency room. I suppose that she could have sued us, but the fall was so obviously an accident and our concern so genuine that there was never any talk about a lawsuit.

THE BENEFITS OF HONESTY

Several months later, during an interview with a reporter, we were asked if any of our students had ever been injured while performing gymnastics. "Yes," we said, and explained what had happened. The reporter not only commended us for doing the right thing, but he also said that few other people would have been as candid as we had been.

In other words, we had won a friend, an influential reporter who had no doubts about our credibility, good will, and responsibility. Those qualities were invaluable, for they enhanced the reputation of our school. In fact, the story was passed along to others throughout the years, and served to impress all who heard it.

ALWAYS MAKE A COMMENT

If something bad happens to you, never say, "No comment." Such responses invariably make you sound guilty. After all, if you have nothing to hide, why are you refusing to answer questions?

Similarly, silence is assumed to be an admission of guilt.

There is always something you can say; however, it is often difficult to come up with a spontaneous statement, one that makes sense and is a credible explanation. At the very least, you can say, "I shall look into it and get back to you as soon as I find out."

Perhaps the best exemplars of spontaneous deflection are successful politicians. When asked embarrassing questions, they find ways of briefly and superficially responding with seeming sincerity. If they have extra reserves of cleverness, they launch into some diversionary tangent, successfully changing the subject to one that is more congenial to them.

The failure to have adequate presence of mind is perhaps best exemplified by those old newspaper photos of gangsters being led away in handcuffs: they have their jackets over their heads, their hats pulled down, and their bodies hunched up. What pictures of guilt! If they were not guilty, or if they wanted to create an impression of being unjustly accused, they would have walked proudly, holding their heads high. And, if they were even better actors, they would have adopted the countenances of suffering martyrs.

I once saw an evening news story about someone who had been arrested after stealing hundreds of thousands of dollars from New York City. As he was being led away in handcuffs, he attempted to kick the video camera out of the hands of the television newsman. As another reporter asked him if he was guilty, Mr. Savoir-faire spit at the reporter.

Not exactly the kind of behavior that will convince a jury of public opinion to hold you in high esteem.

Even John Gotti used to walk into court as the most self-confident man in the world. He swaggered and smiled as if he were going to a party as the honored guest.

Meyer Lansky, a gangster from an earlier era, never used to run away from the press. In fact, while living in Miami Beach, he would walk his tiny dog, Bruzzer; when television reporters would run over to him and ask questions (the answers to which would have made his life more troublesome than it was), he would walk right towards the reporters and their cameras. He would simply smile and say, "You fellas sure are good at walking backwards. I've gotta try that sometime."

He had, in effect, changed the subject, smiling about the reporters' unusual skills in being able to ask questions while walking backwards. The little old man out with his dog seemed to be no more than someone's kindly grandfather—just the image he wanted to portray.

Now if two notorious criminals can have sufficient presence of mind to avoid indicting themselves in the media, so can most other people.

NEVER DENY SOMETHING THAT YOU HAVE NOT BEEN ACCUSED OF

As I wrote earlier, it is bad enough to put negative publicity in a spotlight, but it is even worse to breathe life into something that is either dead or not an issue at all. Such was the case with Richard Nixon who, while suffering the slings and arrows of the Watergate investigation, announced on national television that he was not a crook. No one had asked if he was a crook. He had enough problems with Watergate; he didn't have to raise an issue that no one else had. As a result of his uncalled-for denial, people wondered if Nixon was a crook in addition to his other failings.

MAKE A FRESH START

Years ago, a client was accused in the press of indulging in certain financial improprieties. He had been the subject of several extremely negative news stories and didn't know what to do about it. He asked someone's advice, and that person suggested he contact me.

When we met, I told him that he had to resign from his high-profile position, and turn over responsibility for the day-to-day running of his company to a respected professional who would be beyond reproach. He agreed; he would stay on as the owner of the company, but he would not write checks, and not be in a position where his presence could hurt the company.

He hired a very bright young woman and put her in charge. I called various reporters and told them what my client had done. They each ran stories that reflected on his good judgment, regardless of how belated it was. The stories also quoted me as the spokesperson for the company.

Three days later, he changed his mind. He fired the woman, took back his presidency, and called the press to tell them that their earlier stories were untrue. He had made me into a public liar, so

I immediately resigned. The press then did stories about him that were just short of public beheadings.

He had succeeded in ruining his reputation. His narcissism had not permitted him to hand over the reins of responsibility to another, especially a woman who was morally upright.

Within a year, however, his presence was dooming his business, and others prevailed upon him to resign. He did, but it was too late. The company failed.

MISTAKE #2: ALIENATING THE MEDIA

Many people think that they should have an adversarial relationship with reporters: they've got to be tough—if not, the reporters will take advantage of them, walk all over them. That is one of the worst things anyone can do, for it means that those who can get your message to potential customers have no desire to help you.

A reporter, in an odd sort of way, is working not just for an employer, but also for you. By reporting favorably about your products/services, that reporter is providing you with valuable credibility that advertising alone will not produce.

I used to be friendly with a young reporter who had broken into journalism by doing celebrity interviews. Her interviews were so solicitous of her subjects that publicists often welcomed her presence. That all changed at a certain point, when she was asked to interview a well-known actress. The actress and her publicist assumed that the journalist would be as solicitous as she had been to her other subjects. The journalist, however, had earned her stripes, and now had something new to prove to more serious journalists who had written her off as a mere cipher. Unfortunately for the actress, she did not know that the journalist had altered her career goals and priorities. It was also unfortunate that the actress had a personality so abrasive that it could take the skin off people who wore their feelings close to the surface. The actress had, for years, positioned herself in the public mind as one whose sympathies naturally ran to all the underprivileged wrecks of the world. In the presence of the no-longer-obeisant reporter, the actress displayed her worst attributes: she screamed at her servants; she threw a bottle of perfume at a wall; she ordered people about as if they were her slaves. So bad was her behavior that she made Marie Antoinette look like a democrat!

The ensuing story, though not as lethal as it could have been, still painted a picture of the actress as a spoiled, temperamental brat in love only with the sounds, smells, and image of herself.

From that point on, whenever the publicist arranged an interview, she submitted a series of questions to interviewers before they met with the actress. They were told in no uncertain terms that only the questions on the sheet of paper that she had supplied would be answered. Not only were interviewers told to stick to the prepared questions, but the answers were as rehearsed as any lines in a script.

It worked.

Though many in the media knew how obnoxious the actress could be, few of her fans ever found out.

HEAR NO EVIL; SPEAK NO EVIL

When I started out in public relations, I worked on behalf of a number of well-known rock bands. There was one band, in particular, that had great stage presence. Its members, however, could not be bothered with the reporters who could be instrumental in making them famous, or even infamous. While all were talented musicians, they were also bratty narcissists, who regarded the world as their playpen.

Every autumn and spring they went on a ten-city tour. My job was to arrange newspaper, radio, and television interviews for them before they arrived in each of the cities. The publicity was simply a device for selling tickets to their concerts several weeks in advance. The band, however, would have no part of my machinations. If the world wanted to hear them, fine. If not, then (to use their brilliant locution), "the public could get stuffed!"

Obviously, they presented me with certain professional obstacles. After a few conversations with colleagues, I found a relatively easy way to tackle the print medium. Though I had attempted to interview each of the bandmembers, all I got for my efforts were grunts and muttered curses and vague mumblings. It was hardly the clever repartee that would sell tickets.

With no other options available and a job to do, I made up answers to my own questions. I gave copies of the helpful interviews to each of the band members, and they more-or-less mumbled their consent to publish the interviews. Many small daily and weekly newspapers published the interviews, along with photos of the band members. Television news interviews, however, posed problems which could not be so easily finessed. After some further investigations, I arranged for film clips of their earlier concerts to be edited into news stories. In some cases, a voice-over reporter read a narrative; in others, the suggested script of a narrative was supplied to local television news programs. Eventually, I located a company that did nothing but create news releases for television, and the company supplied a more sophisticated version of what I have just described. Radio was even simpler, for it consisted simply of audiotaped news releases.

These two cases of not perceiving the media as helpful are merely examples of what you should avoid.

MISTAKE #3: SENDING PRESS RELEASES TO THE WRONG PEOPLE

There are many people in the media who report on your business. If you send press releases to them, you will—at the very least—alert them to the nature of your business.

When sending a press release make sure you send it to the correct reporter or editor. If you don't know who that person is, then call the newspaper, magazine, or radio or television station, and ask who should receive your information. In many cases, you can get away with sending your press release to the city editors at newspapers, to the assignment editors at television news programs, and to the news directors at radio stations. While that approach may result in your message landing on the desk of the appropriate person, it is no substitute for developing personal relations with such people. Picking up a telephone and initiating a conversation with a reporter or editor may be the first step in the development of a friendship, one that will pay valuable dividends throughout the years.

Not long ago, I was having dinner with a reporter in New York. While sipping wine, he told me that too much of his time was wasted on getting phone calls from people who wanted him to publicize something that was of no interest to him.

"Why don't such people call my editor and ask who reports on fashion, or food, or new restaurants? They just see my name on a story, like the story, and think I will want to write about them. Or maybe, they simply want me to write about them. They could save themselves a lot of time if they just found out who they should send their stories to."

ALWAYS MAKE FOLLOW-UP PHONE CALLS

This brings me to a second point of some importance: you should always make a follow-up phone call to the person to whom you have sent your press release. You not only want to know if that person received it, but you also want to know if it is of interest. If your story was lost or misplaced, you can send another copy. If your story is not of interest, you can ask why. From the response, you can learn what's wrong, what's right, and make appropriate changes. Perhaps you emphasized something that was not newsworthy, and concentrated on something that was trivial.

181

SHARPEN THE FOCUS OF YOUR PRESS RELEASES

Without falsifying stories, you can refocus your emphasis and make a story newsworthy.

In Chapter 2, for example, I wrote about a press release for Check-a-Mate investigations that dealt with short men cheating on their wives more than tall men do. I simply emphasized one aspect of a story that Check-a-Mate had told me. I did not falsify the facts; I merely found that aspect of the story that was unusual and humorously newsworthy. A reporter can often help you to see what is newsworthy and what is not.

Speaking with reporters, however, should not become a substitute for writing focused press releases, and you should not ask them to do your job for you. If, however, you send a press release to a reporter, and they find it lacking, you can ask why. Their answers, if they are willing to respond, will help you to create a story that the reporter finds of interest. Of course, once a reporter has helped you, they have invested time and interest in you and, chances are, will want to see that your story gets published.

MISTAKE #4: TRYING TO "GET EVEN" AFTER NEGATIVE PUBLICITY

If the media doesn't report what you want it to, or you get negative publicity, don't try to get even. Some large companies even threaten to cancel their advertising. It rarely works.

Instead, you will do a lot better if you alter your marketing program to get the results you want.

If you expect to market your products and services for many years, you will need the help of the media. While it may be good advice in some places not to get mad, but to get even, that advice should be reversed when dealing with the media. Get mad, maybe even make your anger known, but don't try to get even. It will backfire, and you will lose potential allies.

MISTAKE #5: NOT TAILORING YOUR MARKETING PROGRAM TO YOUR CUSTOMERS

One of the most common mistakes of the neophyte marketer is not to tailor a marketing and public relations program to the interests of potential customers. Time and again, I have seen people tailor programs that reflect their tastes, their conceptions, and their values. A reporter gets the information, looks it over, and tosses it into the trash. A consumer is alerted to your offer, but is not interested and spends money someplace else.

If you want to make people ingredients in your success, you must appeal to their self-interest. And there is no better way than speaking with them before you commence a marketing public relations program.

ASK THE MEDIA

You may want to begin by making a list of local reporters and editors. Call and introduce yourself to each of them. Tell them what you are planning and ask if they find it of interest. Ask what specifically interests them about it. Ask them what materials they would like to receive. Ask them if they would look over some preliminary information that you will be happy to send. Some reporters, of course, will be too busy to give you much help. Others, however, may be genuinely interested and do whatever little they can to be of assistance. You should, of course, repay their favors by taking them out to lunch or dinner. Indeed, such behavior could be the beginning of numerous friendships, ones that will provide you with many professional advantages.

SET UP A FOCUS GROUP

Next, you should assemble at least ten people into a focus group. You will probably have to pay them, or give them free products.

Once you have gotten them together, you want to find out what they think about your products/services. What do they like, what do they not like? How would they make improvements?

If it's a food product, let's say, you can ask them about the design of the package, the colors of the package, the shape and size of the container in which you have put the product. You can ask if they prefer glass, plastic, cardboard, or tin. You can then go on to the product itself, asking them to taste it. Is it spicy enough, does it require more salt, do they like the way it feels in their mouths? The questions, obviously, can go on and on. At the end of the process, especially if you use several different focus groups, you will have gained all the insights you require to create a product that consumers will find irresistible.

NO ONE IS AN ISLAND

Prior to opening my own public relations and marketing company, I was asked by my boss to accompany him to a garment manufacturer. The man had been in business for twenty years; he had taken five years to build a comfortably successful business, but then sales began falling. By his twentieth year, he was desperate. Sales were so poor that he could only meet his expenses. There were no profits.

After having spoken with him for a few minutes about his business, we asked him why he thought everything was turning to ashes.

"Everyone hates me," cried the dress manufacturer. "People won't buy from me, because they hate me. I don't know why, and I don't know what to do about it. That's why I called you."

We asked him if we could speak with his former customers and those in the marketplace who might be his new customers.

"Go ahead. Speak to whoever you want, for all the good it'll do."

He gave us a list of people, and we conducted systematic interviews with each. We learned that many of his former customers had grown old, retired, or died. Those who were still doing business said they didn't hate our client; rather, he had lost touch with their needs. He never asked what they wanted or what would sell, whereas other manufacturers eagerly accommodated themselves to the marketplace, and so they dealt with those others. Our client, when he burst upon the scene, had been something of a wunderkind. He had bet right on the money at the beginning, but then the market had changed, and he hadn't changed with it. He was waiting for the marketplace to come to him, as it had in the past, and he did not go to it. It was remarkable, considering his point of view, that he even called us.

When we interviewed potential customers, those with whom he had never done business, we learned that they didn't hate him. They didn't know he existed! That was a blow to his ego that really made him sit up in his chair.

If he hadn't reached a level of desperation, he never would have contacted us, and we would not have been able to help him save his business.

It is said of alcoholics that they must "hit bottom" before they can reform their lives. That manufacturer almost hit bottom, and was smart enough to go the marketplace with his ideas before he went there with his products. With that knowledge, he was able to create garments he could sell and so restore his business to financial health.

PATIENCE AND PERSISTENCE

Once you have learned to avoid the most common mistakes in marketing your products, you must also learn that patience and persistence are essential ingredients for breeding success. Without those two ingredients, success will never be yours.

I have seen countless clients possessed of impatience for success—it infects them like a virus. I explain to them that achieving success is little different from investing in the stock market: you choose your investments carefully, then you watch your investments grow.

Whatever time you put into marketing a business is an investment of time and effort; it rarely reaps substantial rewards immediately. Marketing is not magic; it's not like pulling a golden rabbit out of a hat. It takes time and patience.

Similarly, a farmer invests in the growth of crops, waters and fertilizes his plants, until one day they are ready for the thresher.

Most marketing efforts that fail do so not because the effort was badly conceived in the first place; rather, they fail because sufficient time and patience were missing from the enterprise.

In a world of instant gratification, there are many people who want their results at the moment that they have finished planning. It would be equivalent to seeing a house build itself immediately after you had completed the blueprints.

FOOD FOR INSTANT GRATIFICATION

Here's an example of such short-sighted thinking; unfortunately, it is all too typical. A client opened a potentially very successful restaurant. He contacted me and asked to put together a marketing and public relations plan; I did so. He began enjoying a slow but steady increase in business. The results were more than dribbling in; each week he was attracting more and more customers.

After four months, I had doubled the size of his business. A number of promotions and publicity-oriented events were getting meaningful results—but not meaningful enough for my client, I soon discovered.

I was planning a direct mail piece offering a special discount program; I had done similar promotions with other restaurants, and each one had proved successful. I wanted to send the piece to every person who lived within the same zip code as the restaurant. In addition, I had set up a wine-tasting event with a local beer and wine distributor, as well as a fashion show with a popular boutique. Altogether, the discount promotion and the two events would have brought in hundreds of new customers; however, he did not want to spend money on the wine, he did not want to advertise the fashion show, he did not want to spend money printing a direct mail piece, and he did not want to spend money on postage, even at bulk mail rates. In other words, he was unwilling to spend money to make money. He didn't want to invest in the success of his restaurant. He thought his unique restaurant was so wonderful that people would flock to it as if it were a religious shrine.

He dispensed with my services, and decided that he would be carried to success and profits on a rising tide of word-of-mouth publicity.

Six months later, he sold the restaurant, because sales had fallen dramatically. The new buyer picked it up at a bargain price and hired me to increase sales.

A MARKETING PROGRAM IS A LONG-TERM INVESTMENT

It took me 15 months to generate the kind of traffic and sales that the new owner had established as his goal. He looked upon the restaurant as an investment, one that would eventually pay high dividends. It did, and it still does.

When people hire me, I always make a point of explaining one essential ingredient: "If you are not prepared to make a long-term commitment to a successful marketing and public relations program, whether with me or someone else, don't even begin. Don't waste your money. If you expect results tomorrow, you will be disappointed."

There are many con artists who will promise prospective clients whatever they believe the prospect wants to hear. They will collect a monthly retainer for a while, get fired, and go on to the next client. Such people create a bad impression about the nature of marketing; however, they wouldn't be able to do so if clients did not insist on instant gratification.

A MARKETING PROGRAM IS LIKE THE STOCK MARKET

One of my more profitable hobbies is investing in the stock market; I have done quite well at it for more than twenty years. I made my first investment when I was a freshman in college: I borrowed $300 to buy shares in a relatively new fast food restaurant: McDonald's. I loved the hot apple pie, and I was sure other people would, too. In two years, I doubled my money.

All my stock picks have been governed by a simple principle: if a company produces and sells products that are of value, then that company's stock will continue to go up. Of course, I also understand that the market can be like a roller coaster ride. If a stock drops precipitously because the market has dropped, I know that both the market and the stock will come back up, especially if the company continues to do well. Stock prices fluctuate, now dropping, now rising, buouyed by unforeseen economic currents. In the long run, I stay with my investments, and each has paid me handsome profits.

I also advise several friends on their stock portfolios. One of these recommended me to one of her friends. I told her friend to call me once a week, and I would let her know what I was buying and selling. She was extremely impatient and called me not just every day, but several times a day. If she purchased a stock on my recommendation, she became anxious if it did not go up the next day. If it did not go up in three or four days, she became agitated. If, after two weeks, it still hadn't gone up, she sounded desperate. Another week of anxious waiting would go by, and she would sell the stock. A year later, one stock, for example, had gone up 20%. She called me and asked why I hadn't convinced her to stick with her investment. I told her I wasn't a psychiatrist, and could not help someone with such a need for instant gratification.

While that woman was obviously a victim of her anxieties, there are many otherwise intelligent people who act similarly about marketing. If one isn't prepared to regard a marketing program as an

188

investment in a blue chip stock, and nurture it with patience, it will never bear fruit.

A SIMPLE FORMULA

I always suggest that clients write down how much money their businesses are generating annually. Thereafter, I submit my annual budget for marketing the client's products/services. At the end of a year, I tell them to write down how much money they have spent for marketing and public relations; to determine that year's increase in sales; and then subtract the marketing costs from the increase in sales. They then see if their investment is paying off. If, for example, their increase is more than 15% above their investment in marketing, they are doing as well as some of the best money managers on Wall Street.

QUICK TIPS FOR SUCCESS

Avoid the mistakes enumerated in this chapter; such common mistakes regularly sink marketing programs. Don't let it happen to you.

And always remember these cardinal rules: Be prepared to make a 100% commitment to your marketing public relations program; be patient yet persistent while pursuing results; invest time and effort into the program. If you are prepared to do all three, you should reap the kinds of rewards that will put a smile on your face as you regularly go to the bank with ever-larger deposits.

CHAPTER 12

Your Marketing Program, Your Press Kit

Now that you have read about the necessary ingredients for successfully marketing and promoting your business, you should create your own effective marketing and public relations program, as well as an informative media kit. The marketing program will be your blueprint for success, and the media kit will provide reporters with the story you want to tell them about your business.

While your marketing program should certainly be your guide to success, you should feel free to deviate from it and to improvise changes that will generate positive results. In other words, after you get your feet wet, let yourself go and be creative.

All successful marketing and promotion campaigns have strong elements of spontaneity, creativity, and improvisation. Your marketing program is, indeed, a blueprint—but one that is not cast in concrete. Instead, it is more like wet clay, and can be changed here and there as circumstances may demand.

THE MARKETING PROGRAM

To begin, identify the market for your products/services. Write this information down. Next, determine if you can expand your market to those who may not have been included in your original calculation. Make a list of the expanded market, too.

ATHLETIC SHOES FOR NON-ATHLETES

Here's an example that may give you some helpful ideas. If you are selling athletic shoes to joggers, runners, and fitness enthusiasts, you might also want to expand your market to include those who do a lot of walking, those who have foot problems and require unusually comfortable shoes, and older people who tend to have more foot problems than younger people.

One could further position athletic shoes as a healthful and comfortable alternative to regular shoes. Consumers can be and, indeed, have been encouraged to wear athletic shoes on weekends, when stylish business dress is unnecessary and comfort is of primary importance.

SUNGLASSES IN THE DARK

The marketing of sunglasses provides another helpful example. Years ago, sunglasses were sold to people primarily as a means of protecting their eyes in bright summer sunshine. Somewhat later, manufacturers of ski equipment realized that sunglasses would be ideal for those skiing down brilliantly glistening snow slopes, where reflected sunlight can be almost blinding. Still later, manufacturers realized that since movie and rock stars wore sunglasses, even in the dead of night, sunglasses could be marketed as glamour items to celebrity wannabes.

POSITIONING YOUR PRODUCT

The success achieved in the aforementioned examples resulted from products being positioned, and repositioned.

Every successful product is positioned. Positioning simply means defining or redefining your products for the tastes of particular marketplaces; the products will, therefore, have specific identities that are meaningful to specific categories of consumers.

POSITIONING FAST FOOD

Fast food offers a good example of successful positioning and repositioning. It was originally positioned for its convenience and low price. After the general population became concerned with calories and saturated fats, however, fast food marketers began to add and promote low-calorie and low-fat meals on their regular menus. Fast food menus had been repositioned to appeal to the trend of healthful eating.

POSITIONING TO A VARIETY OF MARKETS

Obviously, the more markets you go after, the greater will be your sales. For an example, one need only look at car companies that make basically the same car, yet give it different names and slightly different lines, and then market it to different groups of consumers. Those markets might include young adults with limited funds who want an economical car, wealthy people who are willing to pay for added-on luxuries, and older people who will be most concerned about comfort, safety, and economics. In all cases, the same basic car can be the starting point. Each will have the same basic engine, the same basic body. Consumers, however, will feel that they have chosen cars that match their specific needs.

POSITIONING TO DIFFERENT CLASSES

About fifteen years ago, one of my neighbors went to Germany and returned home with a slightly used Mercedes Benz. He bought the car abroad because it cost only a third of what he would have had to pay for it in the United States. He simply drove it around Germany, making it a slightly used car, thus avoiding the special duties for importing a new car into the U.S.

In Germany, his model of Mercedes was a solid middle-class car with a middle-class price tag; in the United States, however, it was positioned as a luxury car, and consumers naturally paid a luxurious price. In other words, it was simultaneously positioned as two different classes of car.

PRODUCTS ARE IN THE EYES OF THE BEHOLDER

In the early 1960s, a swanky Madison Avenue jewelry store purchased small cocktail handbags from a retailer who could not sell them. The store paid $1.00 for each of the bags, and sold each bag for the then-exorbitant price of $50! It was able to do so because the bags were positioned as elegant accessories that all chic women should own. The price of $50 made the bags seem even more elegant and chic than bags selling for much less.

FROM ETHNICITY TO HEALTHFULNESS

Here's an example of successful positioning to expand one's market. At one time, Bertolli Olive Oil (and all olive oil) was perceived as belonging to an ethnic food category. However, medical research discovered that olive oil contains monounsaturated fats, which are not only more healthful than saturated fats, but are even more healthful than other unsaturated fats. Saturated fats increase cholesterol that may result in atherosclerosis in veins and arteries, while polyunsaturated fats contribute very little to that condition. Mono-unsaturated fats go even further: such fats may help to dissolve the fatty deposits in veins and arteries. Once that information could be publicized, olive oil no longer had to be positioned simply as an ethnic food—it could be repositioned as a tasty health-food product. As a result, the shelf space for olive oil dramatically increased, and sales went through the roof.

IDENTIFYING CUSTOMER BENEFITS

Why would a consumer want to buy your products or use your services? If consumers are going to buy your products or use your services, they must be able to enumerate several advantages that set your products/services apart from the competition. Make a list of benefits that consumers will value. Appeal to their self-interest. Are any of the benefits unique?

You should also try to tie benefits to your specific market.

A Super Scissor For The Loss Of Flexibility

For example, Professional Foot Care Products created a unique product called the Super Scissor. It has a 5″-long shank so that older people, who have less flexibility than younger people, will not have to bend as far when cutting their toenails. It is unique; there is no other scissor like it. It is marketed to older people through magazines that are read by people over the age of 65. In addition, the product is placed among other products that have value to senior citizens.

WRITING YOUR MARKETING PLAN

Now it is time to write out your marketing plan. It should be brief and to the point. In simple, clear sentences, answer the following questions; the questions will serve as an outline for your plan, and the answers will be the plan.

1. Who makes up the market for my products/services?
2. Can I market my products/services to a larger group of consumers than those in number 1?
3. If so, what groups make up that market?
4. How will I position my products/services? When will I start?
5. To which markets will that positioning be directed?
6. Can I list the benefits of my products/services? (If so, make a list in order of importance.)
7. Can I list the reasons consumers will want to buy my products/services? (If so, list those reasons, in order of importance.)
8. When will I reach my market? What will my prices be?
9. How will I reach my market?
    a. Newspapers—dailies or weeklies?
    b. Magazines—monthlies or weeklies?
    c. Radio
    d. Television
10. Which of the following will I use; when, and to what extent?
    a. Advertising
    b. Publicity
    c. Direct mail
    d. Telemarketing
    e. Signage
    f. Trade shows, fairs, seminars
11. What percentage of my gross sales should I spend on marketing? What kind of return do I want on my investment?

There are no hard and fast rules about how much you should spend. It should be no more than enough to get results; however, you should be prepared to spend money on marketing regularly and consistently for at least six months.

Many of your financial decisions will be based not only on your budget, but on your level of comfort. Obviously, that varies from person to person.

As your business and its profits grow, you will certainly be able to increase the amount of money you earmark for promotions. As you increase your marketing budget, you should realize a concomitant increase in sales and profits.

Remember that the plan you make today will probably have to be altered in a month, and then altered again. It is important to be flexible and creative, to be opportunistic, and to take advantage of every market change.

CHOOSE YOUR MEDIA CONTACTS

Make a list of all media outlets that you will use to promote your business. After you have made lists of newspapers, magazines, and radio and television programs, you should also make a list of editors, reporters, and talk show hosts who regularly deal with products/services that are similar to your own.

If you are going to use media outlets for advertising, then request their media kits, which will provide you with demographics and frequency costs for advertising.

The most complete media guides for your press releases are *Bacon's Newspapers*; *Magazines*; *Radio*; and *Television*; and *New York Publicity Outlets*. You can buy these directories, or consult them in libraries. In an appendix, I have provided the addresses and telephone numbers of their publishers.

While you should be flexible and creative, you must nevertheless commit yourself to marketing and stick to your commitment. Your commitment will spell the difference between success and failure. If your competition is succeeding, they are marketing and promoting their businesses. If you don't do the same, the competition will overwhelm you.

THE MEDIA KIT

If you are going to use the media to help you market your products/services, you will need a media kit. It tells the story of your business; it will, in effect, be your introduction to reporters and editors who will use it as reference material.

A media kit is a folder large enough to contain sheets that are $8\frac{1}{2}'' \times 11''$ and photos that are $8'' \times 10''$. Exhibit 12-1 shows the cover of the media kit I created for Hill Street Security & Investigations, Inc., which owns Check-a-Mate. When opened, the folder should have two inside pockets, one on each side. Place photos or other visual reproductions in one pocket, printed material in the other pocket.

The following items should be included in your media kit:

1. A bio of you that is at least one page in length, but certainly no more than two pages. The bio should contain the following information:

   a. Relevant education
   b. If married, a statement of that fact and spouse's name
   c. Number of children
   d. Awards
   e. Current position
   f. Previous relevant positions
   g. Organizations to which you belong
   h. If you are promoting yourself as a professional, a black and white glossy photo of yourself

Exhibit 12-2 is the bio of Jerry Palace, who runs Check-a-Mate.

2. A description of your business:

   a. What it does
   b. Why it was started; when it was started
   c. What makes it different or unique

Exhibit 12-3 shows an example.

EXHIBIT 12-1 Media kits introduce your business to reporters and editors who can then use the information to promote your business. This exhibit shows the cover for the Hill Street Security & Investigations, Inc. media kit.

EXHIBIT 12-2 It is a good idea to include your bio in your media kit. Here is an example of Jerry Palace's brief but informative bio.

From: Jeffrey Sussman, Inc.
Marketing Public Relations
249 East 48 Street
New York, N.Y. 10017

For: Check-a-Mate, a division of
Hill Street Security & Investigations

Contact: Jeffrey Sussman
(212) 421-4475

JERRY PALACE: DEDICATION IN THE PURSUIT OF TRUTH & JUSTICE

Jerry Palace grew up in the Bronx. While other members of his family had been outstanding cops, it was his father who gave Jerry a sense of right and wrong: it was his father who had fought in the United States Infantry in World War II. He had survived one of the worst encounters of that good war, the Battle of the Bulge. He understood the importance of being at the right place at the right time, and that was one of the things he taught his son. It was his father's example that finally encouraged Jerry to become a cop. During his eighteen years as a uniformed police officer and as a detective, Jerry served the South Bronx with a dedication that was rewarded with more than thirty commendations. He served in a high-profile, often dangerous Anti-Crime Unit whose members were often exposed to some of the city's most dangerous street criminals. In addition, he went undercover in a narcotics unit, where he often posed as a buyer in order to make risky arrests, some of which could have ended in his death. For his last five years on the force, Detective Palace served in a highly acclaimed robbery unit, which led him to apprehension of one of the leaders of the notorious Purple Gang.

EXHIBIT 12-2 (continued)

Jerry Palace is the father of four daughters, ranging in ages from two through fourteen. He lives with his wife in Westchester County, N.Y.

EXHIBIT 12-3 A description of your business should also be part of your media kit. Here, Check-A-Mate's description includes facts about when and why the business was started, what it does and what makes it unique and different.

From: Jeffrey Sussman, Inc.
          Marketing Public Relations
          249 East 48 Street
          New York, N.Y. 10017

For: Check-a-Mate, a division of
       Hill Street Security & Investigations

Contact: Jeffrey Sussman
            (212) 421-4475

FOR IMMEDIATE RELEASE

DETECTIVE CHECKS ON MATES

Let's say you're a woman who has just met the man of your dreams, but there is something about him that makes you wonder: Does he have another girlfriend? Is he married? Is he after your money? Your apartment? Is he a drug addict? Does he have a criminal record? Is he a child molester?

Such questions frequently plague many single women, which is why Jerry Palace, a retired New York City Detective, runs Check-a-Mate, a service that will thoroughly investigate the backgrounds of prospective spouses, or just the person you may have decided to date on a regular basis.

Mr. Palace has been asked to look into the backgrounds of numerous individuals. "On one occasion," he stated, "I checked

EXHIBIT 12-3 (continued)

into the background of an elegant woman who claimed she had been an actress and a model. Her fiancé, a young investment banker, was doubtful, and so he hired us. It turned out she had been a call girl for eight years." On another occasion, a man and a woman each hired Check-a-Mate to check on one another. "Thank God, neither of them had any skeletons in their closets," commented Palace.

His most recent case was for a woman who believed she was dating a gangster. "The man carried a gun," noted Palace, "and my client was frightened that he might be using it for illegal purposes. Well, I did a complete check on him, and he turned out to be a successful businessman who carried large sums of money. He had a license for the gun and a completely clean record."

What does Check-a-Mate look into when doing a background check? Prior marriages, financial records, a persons's lifestyle, character, personal property, criminal record, military record, business colleagues, and friends—to name the most common areas.

"These days, the most common concerns," noted Palace, "are whether a person has a criminal record, has AIDS, is on the verge of bankruptcy, or is a child molester. That last is particularly frightening to divorced or widowed women with small children. And the notoriety that such deviants have been getting has pushed the issue to the forefront in the minds of many people. Thus far, I have not come across any such cases; however, there are plenty of others I have investigated who have had many other problems, which would make your hair stand on end. I guess I have saved a number of people from getting involved with human disasters."

Check-a-Mate is a division of Hill Street Security & Investigations. It regularly performs marital and premarital investigations, and has done so for people from virtually every walk of life.

3. Product information:

  a. A list of all products, their purposes, and suggested retail prices

  b. $5'' \times 7''$ or $8'' \times 10''$ photos of each product. Photos should be black and white glossies for newspapers, and color for most magazines.

4. If you are introducing products, your media kit should contain new product press releases. Each release should contain a physical description of the product and suggested retail prices.

5. There should be at least one press release with a news story that the media will find of interest, and will use as a basis for a news story. Exhibit 12-4 shows an example.

EXHIBIT 12-4 Your media kit should include at least one press release about your business which the media will find of interest. This exhibit shows such a press release.

From: Jeffrey Sussman, Inc.
        Marketing Public Relations
        249 East 48 Street
        New York, N.Y. 10017

For: Check-a-Mate, a division of
       Hill Street Security & Investigations

Contact: Jeffrey Sussman
           (212) 421-4475

FOR IMMEDIATE RELEASE

10 TELLTALE SIGNS THAT YOUR SPOUSE IS UNFAITHFUL

You've got a certain feeling, an anxiety that something is not right. You may even suspect that your spouse has taken a new lover. How to be sure? Coming right out and asking will only elicit a

EXHIBIT 12-4 (continued)

lie. Before you call your lawyer (suggests Jerry Palace, who runs Check-a-Mate, a private investigative service that checks up on errant spouses), ask yourself the following questions:

1. Are you having less sex with your spouse than is normal for you? Palace says that diminished sexual activity at home may be a sign that your spouse is having sex out of the home.

2. Has your spouse's personality undergone a change? Something has caused it, and it may be the presence of a new lover.

3. Has your spouse less money to spend? "If that person hasn't suffered a financial loss, then the money may be going to pay for dates, dinners, dances, etc.," warns Palace.

4. Has your spouse recently begun devoting an inordinate amount of time to grooming, to worrying about dieting, and to buying new clothing? "Such concerns," says Palace, "indicate a preoccupation with appearance in an effort to impress someone."

5. Is your spouse absent from home more than is usual? If so, where is that person spending time? And with whom?

6. Does your spouse return home and mention new friends who you do not know? Are you never permitted to meet those new friends?

7. If you ask about out-of-the-ordinary changes in behavior, are you told to "mind your own business"? Or are you met with a stonewalling denial? Such obvious attempts at a cover-up are obvious tip-offs that something is wrong.

8. Have you recently received phone calls to which there is no answer when you pick up the phone? Is your spouse making more outgoing calls than can be explained?

9. Does your spouse exhibit new interest in going to such places as art galleries, the ballet, or the opera? If so, it

EXHIBIT 12-4 (continued)

may mean that someone has recently played an important role in altering tastes.

10. Does your spouse show less interest in such responsibilities as the welfare of your children, the appearance of your home, and making financial plans for the future?

"If you can answer yes to 80% of these questions, and you can discount physical illness, or such problems as depression or chronic anxiety, your spouse may very well be having an affair," says Palace.

Just to make sure, you may want to hire an effective and discreet investigation agency, such as Check-a-Mate, which has been featured on numerous television talk shows and news magazine programs.

---

6. Clipped to the outside of your media kit, there should be a one-page covering letter that describes who you are, what you do, and the contents of the attached media kit.
7. One of the inside pockets should have a cut-out for the placement of a business card. Make sure you include a business card.

PROMOTE YOUR BUSINESS TO THE TOP!

You are now ready to market and promote your business. Here's to your success, and the power of your marketing promotions!

APPENDIX

PUBLIC RELATIONS AND MARKETING RESOURCES

Magazines

1. *Adweek*
   1515 Broadway
   New York, NY 10036
   (212) 536-5336

2. *Business Marketing*
   740 North Rush Street
   Chicago, IL 60611
   (312) 649-5260

3. *Creative*
   37 West 39 Street
   New York, NY 10018
   (212) 840-0160

4. *DM News*
   19 West 21 Street
   New York, NY 10010
   (212) 741-2095

5. *Brandweek*
   1515 Broadway
   New York, NY 10036
   (212) 536-5336

6. *Incentive*
355 Park Avenue South–5th floor
New York, NY 10010
(212) 592-6453

7. *P-O-P Times*
2000 North Racine
Chicago, IL 60614
(312) 281-3400

8. *Target Marketing Magazine*
401 North Broad Street
Philadelphia, PA 19108
(215) 238-5300

Directories

1. *New York Publicity Outlets*
P.O. Box 1197
New Milford, CT 06776
(203) 354-9361

2. *Bacon's Information, Inc.*
332 South Michigan Avenue
Chicago, IL 60604
(312) 922-2400

      a. *Bacon's Newspaper Directory*
      b. *Bacon's Magazine Directory*
      c. *Bacon's Radio Directory*
      d. *Bacon's TV/Cable Directory*
      e. *Bacon's Media Calendar Directory*
      f. *Bacon's International Media Directory*
      g. *Bacon's Business Media Directory*

Mailing List Companies

1. Dun & Bradstreet Information Services
   (800) 234-3867

2. Standard & Poor's Corporation
   (212) 208-8000

3. Dunhill International List Co., Inc.
   (212) 686-3700

4. Hugo Dunhill Mailing Lists, Inc.
   (212) 682-8030

Index